T0067895

DESIGNING EFFECTIVE

BIBLICAL INSTRUCTION

CHRIS COBB

WESTBOW
PRESS®
A DIVISION OF THOMAS NELSON
& ZONDERVAN

Copyright © 2017 Chris Cobb.

All rights reserved. No part of this book may be used or reproduced by any means, graphic, electronic, or mechanical, including photocopying, recording, taping or by any information storage retrieval system without the written permission of the author except in the case of brief quotations embodied in critical articles and reviews.

Scripture quotations marked NIV are taken from the Holy Bible, New International Version. NIV. Copyright 1973, 1978, 1984 by International Bible Society. Used by permission of Zondervan. All rights reserved.

Scripture quotations marked HCSB are from the Holman Christian Standard Bible. HCSB. Copyright 1999, 2000, 2002, 2003 by Holman Bible Publishers. Used by permission. Holman Christian Standard Bible, Holman CSB, and HCSB are federally registered trademarks of Holman Bible Publishers.

WestBow Press books may be ordered through booksellers or by contacting:

WestBow Press
A Division of Thomas Nelson & Zondervan
1663 Liberty Drive
Bloomington, IN 47403
www.westbowpress.com
1 (866) 928-1240

Because of the dynamic nature of the Internet, any web addresses or links contained in this book may have changed since publication and may no longer be valid. The views expressed in this work are solely those of the author and do not necessarily reflect the views of the publisher, and the publisher hereby disclaims any responsibility for them.

Any people depicted in stock imagery provided by Thinkstock are models, and such images are being used for illustrative purposes only. Certain stock imagery © Thinkstock.

ISBN: 978-1-5127-9273-7 (sc)
ISBN: 978-1-5127-9272-0 (hc)
ISBN: 978-1-5127-9274-4 (e)

Library of Congress Control Number: 2017910388

Print information available on the last page.

WestBow Press rev. date: 8/15/2017

ACKNOWLEDGMENTS

The heart of this book has been almost ten years in the making, and its completion would not have been possible without the support and encouragement of my wife and children. They are my greatest cheerleaders, and I will always be grateful for them. I also want to thank my parents for their continued support of my ministry. I am additionally indebted to the many undergraduate and graduate professors who have not only taught me how to study God's Word but also how to design effective biblical instruction. This includes the faculty members of Central Bible College, Rocky Mountain Bible Institute, Global University, Colorado Christian University, Denver Seminary, and Southeastern Baptist Theological Seminary. I will never be the same because of their commitment to higher education. I also want to thank the many pastors and mentors that have also supported me and helped me become the man I am today. Lastly, I want to thank Dr. Kenneth Coley for providing the Foreword, and Jeff Crawford and Anissa Labrador, who contributed some of their original material to this book. Thank you everyone, and to God be the glory for the great things he has done!

CONTENTS

LIST OF FIGURES AND TABLES

Figures

Tables

FOREWORD

For the past two decades, I have had the opportunity to introduce ministry leaders to the concepts of educational leadership presented in this text, *Designing Effective Biblical Instruction*. When I introduce to these educators and ministers the word *curriculum* and its etymology from the Latin word for *racecourse*, I am frequently confronted with blank stares (the author of this book being one of the exceptions, of course). In an effort to connect the unfamiliar with prior learning, I enthusiastically compare this concept with the chariot races in the Colosseum in Rome. More blank stares. You know, like the race in *Ben-Hur*, followed by more stares and the question: Ben who?

Now that the film has been updated and widely publicized, I hope the movie reference gives us a place to start as I make claims about the significance of instructional design-both the concepts and this text. Like the chariot races or today's NASCAR auto races, the Colosseum event had a specific beginning place, a prescribed course laid out, and a designated finish line; at which point, there was always an evaluation. And who finishes first and in what order others follow is never viewed indifferently.

These three characteristics-a starting point, a path to follow, and an end point where assessment takes place-tell you all you need to know about the importance of this text for you and your ministry leadership. Let's be straight. Most ministry leaders, if they are being honest, do not have a firm grasp on any of these three ingredients in their ministry planning. They begin a new season of discipleship with the latest and newest "hot item" from online shopping or the local bookstore with little or no information about their congregants' backgrounds and abilities. But they drop the flag, and the participants are off. But wait a moment. Did we ever stop to consider whether or not the writers of the curriculum resource have a clue about the makeup of our classes? (Chapter 1 examines this.) How about the ability levels and prior learning of our disciples? (Chapter 2). How about our ministry's overall goals? (Chapter 3). How could even the best intentioned author in a different state and maybe even a different culture know much about the spiritual race of my athletes? (Chapter 4).

Dr. Chris Cobb cares deeply about ministry leaders taking back the decision-making and race course design from publishers and writers. But he also is aware that those who oversee educational/discipleship programs lack the specific training necessary to make this happen. Ben who? Designing what?

If I may, let's switch metaphors to assembling a five-hundred-piece puzzle. The author and I are concerned that those who are mentoring new believers, leading discipleship, or teaching a formal Bible class have no "box top" to guide their instructional plans. Present in their heads are glorious insights about the reality of Christ and the truth found in Scripture. But there is missing a prescribed format for arranging these puzzle pieces. Which pieces do I reveal first and in what order? In chapter 5, the concepts of determining the breadth of what is to be covered and in what order the pieces are examined are discussed. Each piece is then assigned an overall objective or target for the teacher and learner to aim at (Chapter 6). After the selection of the pieces is made, placed in a logical order and the objectives determined, the next significant question is asked: what instructional activities will most effectively aid comprehension and memory retention? (Chapter 7). Finally, each leader-teacher must ask: did we get there? To what extent did my learners grasp the big ideas? (Chapter 8).

When I consider my career in teaching and leading, I continue to be inspired by Colossians 1:28 (HCSB). "For we proclaim Him, warning and teaching everyone with all wisdom, so that we may present everyone mature in Christ." I believe that you share this passion with the apostle Paul—to present your students mature in Christ. But I think you will agree, this maturity is not going to be achievable if we, as teachers, have a haphazard approach to our preparation and planning. In this text, Dr. Cobb provides you a committed leader-teacher, with the guidance that you need to oversee effectively the design of the instructional activities the Lord has called you to. I challenge you to dedicate yourself to putting the concepts described in the following pages into practice in your ministry.

Kenneth S. Coley, EdD

PREFACE

I recently attended a prominent Christian education conference, and one of the keynote speakers there described an experience he had as a youth pastor. His church was connected to a Christian school, and one year he was asked by the school's administration to step in and teach a couple of Bible classes temporarily as they had lost their teacher unexpectedly. Unsure of whether or not he should accept the additional responsibilities, he told the leaders of that school, "I was a Bible major in college. I have no idea about education."

I don't know about you, but I can relate to this pastor's sentiment as I reflect on my early years in educational ministry. I too felt unqualified to teach even though I had a bachelor's degree in Bible and theology. Sure, I took an education class as part of my degree program, but I had little expertise when it came to developing a series of lessons, assessing the people in my educational ministry, or incorporating a wide range of teaching strategies. I was mostly trained in hermeneutics and homiletics, not education. When I entered the ministry, I had to write much of the material that I taught, but I didn't feel equipped with the necessary training to do this effectively.

After several years of trying to figure it out on my own, I decided to pursue a master's degree at Colorado Christian University (CCU) in curriculum and instructional design. While this program was designed for general education (K–12) teachers, I quickly discovered that the skills I was acquiring through each course directly applied to biblical instruction. To help me put these new concepts in practice, I not only continued teaching in my local church, but I also found a Christian school where I could teach Bible classes on a part-time basis. I enjoyed my initial experience so much that I have continued doing so off and on for the past decade.

My experiences and studies at CCU (followed by Denver Seminary and Southeastern Baptist Theological Seminary) have spurred on my desire to write this book. Through the years, I come to believe that as stewards of God's Word, we must commit to focusing more on the whole process of instruction. This includes coming to understand the abilities and needs of students, writing succinct goals and objectives, selecting and sequencing material appropriately, choosing relevant teaching strategies, and designing appropriate assessments. This holistic view of the educational process is what is commonly referred to as instructional design. Concentrating on these areas will enable us to better assist our students in retaining and applying the material we share with them.

While there are already many great books available on instructional design (many of which are discussed in this book), few give attention to the needs of pastors and other biblical instructors. In fact, most of the books that are on the market today about instructional design are written from a secular point of view. Books such as Smith and Ragan's (2005) *Instructional Design*, or Dick, Carey, and Carey's (2011) *The Systematic Design of Instruction*, or even Morrison, Ross, Kalman, Kemp's *Designing Effective Instruction* (2011) will give educators a detailed overview of the process of instructional design while giving practical advice for applying its principles in the public school system. However, these textbooks are lengthy, and each author's technical language can make it difficult for many pastors or other biblical instructors to understand its content. Moreover, the authors give no advice for ministers of the gospel who seek to apply these principles in their specific educational ministry.

Seeking to simply the process, Richards and Bredfeldt (1998) wrote an intelligent Christian education textbook entitled *Creative Bible Teaching* that focuses on how Christian educators can write comprehensive lesson plans that take into account learner characteristics, a needs assessment, and a plethora of learning strategies. Richards classic strategy called "hook, book, look, took" has helped countless educators stay focused on the major elements of a lesson. However, this text concentrates solely on individual lesson plans instead of looking at them through the lens of an entire unit or course. Similarly, Clark, Johnson, and Sloat's (1991) collaborative effort in *Christian Education: Foundations for the Future* gives Christian educators an overview of many aspects of education, but they fall short when it comes to teaching people how to develop units of study. Leroy Ford's (1991) astute work entitled *A Curriculum Design Manual for Theological Education* comes closer yet, but its emphasis is more on preparation for collegiate studies.

That is why this current work seeks to pull together both worlds (secular and sacred) to give pastors, small group leaders, Sunday school teachers, and/or Christian school Bible teachers an overview of the instructional design process and how to apply its principles to a number of educational contexts. I hope you will come to enjoy studying these concepts and principles as much as I have, and you will be able to integrate them in your educational ministry as you seek to more effectively teach those whom God has entrusted you with.

1
INTRODUCTION

In their ministry, expositors serve as builders of bridges as they endeavor to span the gulf between the Word of God and the concerns of men and women. To do this they must be as familiar with the needs of their churches as they are with the content of their Bibles.

—Hadden Robinson

My people, hear my teaching; listen to the words of my mouth. I will open my mouth with a parable; I will utter hidden things, things from of old—things we have heard and known, things our ancestors have told us. We will not hide them from their descendants; we will tell the next generation the praiseworthy deeds of the Lord, his power, and the wonders he has done.

—Psalm 78:1–4 (NIV)

"That was a great series!"
"You really challenged me today."
"You knocked it out of the park with that one!"
"I always learn so much from your lessons."

Who wouldn't love to receive compliments like these after spending countless hours preparing for, and then presenting, a series of biblical lessons or messages? However, as flattering as these

1

comments may sound, they fail to give us as pastors, small group leaders, or Bible teachers any tangible information about how well those in our educational ministries are retaining and applying the content we present. If we do not gauge this on a regular basis, we will fail to understand if the concepts we teach are merely going in one ear and out the other. Since our goal in Christian education is life transformation, we must do our best to ensure our students are following through with what we are communicating.

How to do this effectively is a question that ministers of God's Word have been asking for centuries. Even in the days of the Old Testament, God's prophets contended with how to get the Israelites to heed God's instruction. Consider Ezekiel as an example. Ezekiel was a prophet during the southern kingdom of Israel's exile in Babylon. The Israelites had been displaced in a foreign land because of their sin, but little had changed in their hearts and minds. They were still full of immorality and apostasy. In Ezekiel 33:31–32 (NIV) God exposed their double-mindedness when he told Ezekiel,

> My people come to you, as they usually do, and sit before you to hear your words, but they do not put them into practice. Their mouths speak of love, but their hearts are greedy for unjust gain. Indeed, to them you are nothing more than one who sings love songs with a beautiful voice and plays an instrument well, for they hear your words but do not put them into practice.

This passage stirs my heart every time I read it. Although Ezekiel was faithful in proclaiming God's words, he had become no more than a good entertainer in the eyes of the Israelites. In fact, as Ralph Alexander (1986) points out, the Israelites listened to Ezekiel because he was amusing and fun to watch, but they did not feel a need to respond to his messages. Unfortunately, this haughty attitude can still be found in many churches and Christian schools today. People in our culture love to be entertained, but they resent being told how to live. This reminds me of the apostle Paul's words in 2 Timothy 4:3 (NIV), "For the time will come when people will not put up with sound doctrine. Instead, to suit their own desires, they will gather around them a great number of teachers to say what their itching ears want to hear."

So what can be done to prevent this attitude from emerging in our Bible-based educational programs? I believe part of the solution involves an application of the adage "Those who fail to plan, plan to fail." One reason our students are often unable to retain and apply important information from our well thought-out lessons is that we don't intentionally plan for them to do so. This is why the principles of instructional design can be so beneficial for biblical instructors. Instructional design offers a process for the planning of instruction that will challenge you to consider your learners' characteristics and needs, the educational goals and objectives for a unit or course, the teaching strategies you will utilize, and the assessments that should accompany student learning. Applying these concepts to your educational ministry can lead to greater retention and spiritual development in your students, as they will be afforded more opportunities to grapple with the content that is being presented.

You may be surprised to learn that you have more experience with instructional design than you realize. For every series of messages or Bible studies that you have created, you probably asked several questions. "What does my group need to hear at this time?" "What will be the main purpose of this series?" "What theme(s) will be communicated through this series?" "How will each lesson develop the big idea of the series?" "How will I know if they actually learned the content I presented?" Questions like these (and more) are what professional instructional designers contend with every day. As a teacher or pastor, or both, your job title might not be "instructional designer," but I can assure you that if you are involved in any form of education, then you will design instruction.

That being said, this introductory chapter is meant to help you understand what instructional design entails and how it relates to curriculum. Attention will be given to the steps or building blocks involved in this educative practice. I will also depict the benefits of instructional design and challenge you to link these concepts to your specific educational ministry so they can make a significant difference in the lives of your students.

Defining Instructional Design

First things first! For those unfamiliar with the term **instructional design**, let me begin by unpacking these two conjoining concepts so you will have a better understanding of what they mean together. On the one hand, *instruction* is an aspect of education that refers to the intentional facilitation of the learning process (Smith and Ragan, 2005). As Dick, Carey, and Carey (2009) recognize, learning involves the acquisition of new knowledge, behaviors, skills, values, preferences, or understanding. Therefore, instruction will include the arrangement of activities and experiences that expedite the learning process. Moreover, instruction will always be geared toward a specific educational goal. Ledford and Sleeman (2002) explain this essential element.

> A critical task in the process of instructional design is to write goals, which meet the needs and interests of learners; for genuine, realistic, learning goals should be written as overtly and concretely as they can be written. Their formulation and application are critical to the instructional process. A goal ought to state the exact aim, purpose, or end to any course of action. The statement is a point of departure from which the more specific and complete operational objectives are developed (p. 4).

On the other side of the coin is the term *design*. This expression is related to the idea of planning. Much like an engineer, an instructional designer will look at perceived problems and systematically design —plan for— a solution. Smith and Ragan (2005) recognize that in addition to planning, instructional designers employ a high level of precision, care, and expertise in the systematic development of instruction. They understand that poor planning may result in serious consequences.

The authors add that the very nature of the word design denotes a certain level of creativity. Just as architectural designers benefit from creativity and imagination so should we as communicators of God's Word. Consider how creative Jesus was as he took seemingly complicated theological subjects and boiled them down to mustard seeds, wedding feasts, lost sheep, goats, pearls, hidden treasure, lamps, and even fig trees. We should be just as creative as we communicate the gospel today.

The research I conducted for my doctoral dissertation confirmed the importance of creativity in the classroom as I examined the factors that influence student biblical literacy. After evaluating 601 Christian high-school students scattered over six states, along with their sixteen collective Bible teachers, I discovered that a student's performance and motivation to learn often will be directly proportional to how creative a teacher is in presenting the material. My hypothesis before I began my research was that teacher qualifications (e.g., being certified as a teacher, holding a degree with a major in Bible) would hold the most weight when it came to influencing student scores on biblical literacy tests. However, I found the opposite to be true. It was actually the implementation of curriculum that made the biggest difference in student scores. Teachers who were more creative and employed active learning techniques had students with the highest scores on the biblical literacy tests (Cobb, 2014).

Smith and Ragan (2005) further this discussion by suggesting several ways teachers can become more creative in their design of instruction. First of all, they indicate that the most effective teachers utilize metaphors, narratives, and visual images that lend a sense of continuity, interest, and wholeness to the whole series of instruction. Jesus was a master at doing this. As someone once said, his word-pictures enabled his listeners to use imagination to prove his points. Second, effective teachers challenge themselves to become consumers of examples of learning environments and instructional materials. In other words, they are willing to see what others are doing successfully to help spur on new ideas. Not that you have to steal the designs of other teachers, but let them inspire you to think out of the box. Finally, successful teachers maintain a strong sense of goals in their overall educational programs. They will always be able to see the forest, despite the trees. With all this in mind, as you reflect on your own educational ministry context, consider how much creativity you find yourself putting into your delivery, promotion, and evaluation.

Now that you have a good idea of what the terms *instruction* and *design* involve, let me briefly discuss how these concepts splice together. As Smith and Ragan (2005) explain, "The term instructional design refers to the systematic and reflective process of translating principles of learning and instruction into plans for instructional materials, activities, information resources, and evaluation" (p. 4). Stated simply, instructional design fuses together differing aspects of education, from the needs of learners to educational goals and objectives, teaching materials/curriculum, methods, and assessments. The design of instruction is implemented systematically, which means your **curriculum** will be arranged in a specific order for a specific reason. Curriculum includes the actual content, materials (e.g., books, videos, presentations, readings), and/or textbooks that you teach from. In some cases, you may end up using a published curriculum that includes a curriculum plan, materials, or even a textbook. However, you may also have times when you need to develop these resources from scratch. That being said, it is important to understand that while curriculum refers to what will be taught, instructional design refers to how it will be taught. Therefore, the purpose of instructional design is to create instructional experiences that make the acquisition of knowledge and skills (curriculum) more palatable for students. In doing so, the outcome of instruction will be more observable and measurable.

Linking Instructional Design and Educational Ministry

One of my professors in Bible college used to say that while the message of the gospel never changes, our methods for explaining the gospel might be amended over time. Whatever the means, our focus should always remain on helping people know and understand the gospel and preparing them to live it out and share it with those around them. However, it is evident that many churches and Christian schools struggle to help their students move from point *A* to point *B* in their knowledge and application of the Bible and theological concepts.

In his book, *Why Nobody Learns Much of Anything at Church: And How to Fix It*, Thom Schultz (1993) postulates that this happens in part because biblical instructors often fail to evaluate their own effectiveness. They are too busy doing the "same old, same old" to question whether or not their teaching methods are actually working. Meanwhile, as Schultz surmises, they continue teaching with "blind disregard for learning" because it is what they know and have always done. Pastors and other Christian educators often assume that if they are teaching, then people are learning, but that is a naïve way of thinking. The truth is, when teachers assume, it's as if they are building everything on sand. Schultz adds, "Teaching good stuff isn't good enough. We must be certain that people are learning good stuff. As teachers, we must realize that knowing our subject matter is not enough. We must know how to enable our students to learn the subject matter and live it" (p. 32).

The question I think we all have to ask ourselves is this: are people really learning what they need to in our educational ministries, or is the information going in one ear and out the other? We can share solid, theologically sound messages or lessons until we are blue in the face, but at the end of the day, did anybody learn anything? Are learners genuinely applying the Scripture to their lives on a regular basis? It will take bold ministers of God's Word to assess whether or not this is actually happening. If it is not, effective standards should be put into place that will ensure learning retention. The principles of instructional design will help you in this pursuit as you take intelligent and intentional steps to assist your students in retaining and applying the concepts you teach.

Before I explain the steps involved in instructional design, let me give you several advantages to utilizing the concepts of instructional design in educational ministry. Firstly, as Smith and Ragan (2005) recognize, instructional design serves as an advocate for the learner. To a large degree, the learner becomes the focus of instruction. Unfortunately, many teachers tend to focus on their own learning style and what "works for them," but instructional design challenges them from the very beginning of preparation to consider the learner at every turn. The needs of the learner should take precedence over the teacher's preferences. Instructional design forces teachers to stand in the place of the learner and try to obtain enough information that will help make sure the content is as clear as possible to the learner.

Secondly, instructional design promotes instruction that is both effective and efficient. Students will be more motivated to learn when they perceive that what we are teaching is both necessary and appropriate for them, at their level. As teachers, we can ensure that we are being effective by continually asking ourselves if we are doing and teaching the right things. Do the results match up to what was needed or desired? On the flipside, we must also remain focused on making sure our instruction is efficient. To do so, we must ask ourselves if we are doing the right things right (Rothwell and Kazanas, 2011). What aspects of our lessons might be unnecessary or even undesired? As Smith and Ragan (2005) point out, efficiency "requires the least possible amount of time necessary for learners to achieve goals" (p. 22). Following through with the steps of instructional design will help us as educators to keep our eyes on the prize and focus on what is really important and do it in the best way possible.

Thirdly, applying the principles of instructional design in your educational ministry will help you discern where you are going and how you will get there. This is something I feel is missing in many Bible-based programs today. Deliberate and focused instructional design will require thinking with the end in mind. Consider what evidence of learning will be required from your students when your course or unit is completed. The challenge in this is to focus first on the desired outcomes from which your lessons will logically follow.

Think about it this way. Have you ever been on a cross-country road trip? I have driven several times between Colorado and Florida, and my wife and I have taken the same course each time. Our first trip was very difficult because we did not know the way or the terrain we would encounter. Add to this the fact that it was wintertime, and the threat of snow and ice was imminent and made the trip more dangerous. Our destination (the goal) was sunny Orlando, Florida. To get from point *A* to point *B* on the map, we had to have clear directions. We did not want to end up in Canada, so we worked from an itinerary to keep us from making a purposeless tour of the United States. Keeping the end in mind, we made our way from each highway and side street as needed. Some roads ended up being closed due to construction, but that didn't stop us; we simply adjusted our plans accordingly. Eventually, we made it to our destination because we kept to the plan. Likewise, instructional design will be your plan that gets those in your educational ministry from point *A* to point *B*. This is why Robert Mager (1984) indicates that at its most basic level, instructional design answers three major questions as described below:

1.) Where are we going? (Considering the destination we desire to get to through instruction).
2.) How will we get there? (Considering the instructional strategy that will help us get to the destination).
3.) How will we know when we've arrived? (Considering the assessments that will inform us whether or not students actually got to the destination).

The content of this book will help you navigate through Mager's three questions as they pertain to educational ministry. In order to do this, I have divided the book into two sections. Part I discusses

Mager's first question, which involves instructional analysis. The first thing teachers must do in this process is survey the characteristics of the learners and the learning environment. Subsequently, they will perform a needs assessment that will inform them of the existing knowledge and performance of students. Once this is completed, teachers will develop the focus of the unit or course by describing the main theme and educational goals involved. These goals should be aligned to the summative assessments that will be performed at the end of the process. Teachers will undoubtedly be confronted with the realization that there's too much information available to cover in any one course or unit. So they must determine the scope and sequence. What content needs to be included, and what should be excluded? In what order should the concepts be presented?

Part II of this book expounds on Mager's second and third questions as they pertain to instructional strategies. This level of design is concerned with individual lesson planning. Here teachers create objectives for each lesson that will include specific conditions, performance, and criteria. Next, teachers will be encouraged to broaden their teaching strategy toolbox. They will develop strategies and procedures for how they will present the content, motivate students, and help those students learn the material. These strategies should be based on what teachers know about their students. Teachers will then develop formative and summative assessments that will allow them to verify if their students are actually understanding and applying the material. Concurrently, teachers will give effective feedback to their students in order to help them move forward in their learning (see figure 1 for an illustration of these building blocks of instructional design).

As you read through each chapter, think about how you can apply these concepts in your educational ministry. To help you in this pursuit, I have included a section entitled "Practice Makes Perfect" at the end of each chapter. These practice worksheets will allow you to integrate the models and theories presented in each chapter.

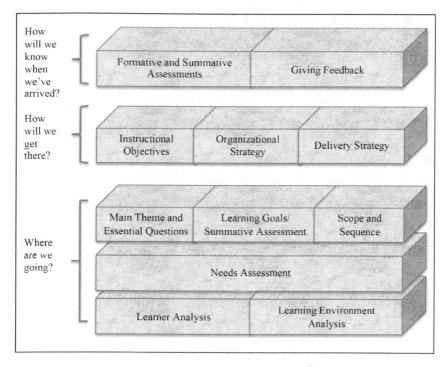

Figure 1: The Building Blocks of Instructional Design

Conclusion

As you begin the journey, I want to commend you for your willingness to go the extra mile as an instructor of God's Word. I recognize that your time is valuable, and I know just how much care you already take in making sure that everything you share with your students is hermeneutically sound and packaged in such a way that everyone within the sound of your voice is positively impacted. My goal through this book is not to add hours to your preparation. Instead, my purpose is to refocus the hours you already spend on preparation. That is why I am an advocate for the team approach when it comes to instructional design and lesson planning. Learn to delegate certain aspects of your design so it will not seem so overwhelming. Work together as a team. It will be worth it!

Lastly, let me challenge you from God's Word because this is the foundation of all our educational ministries. In Matthew 7:24–25

(NIV) Jesus says, "Therefore everyone who hears these words of mine and puts them into practice is like a wise man who built his house on the rock. The rain came down, the streams rose, and the winds blew and beat against that house; yet it did not fall, because it had its foundation on the rock." In this passage, Jesus confirms that those who heed God's Word will not falter when the storms of life come. Instead, their feet will be planted firmly on the Rock of their salvation. I believe that this is something that every Christian should understand, and it should be our goal as Christian educators to help them understand it. My hope and prayer is that God will give those in your educational ministry an insatiable hunger and zeal to learn and apply God's Word. May they be known like Job who said, "I have treasured the words of his mouth more than my daily bread" (Job 23:12b, NIV).

Sources

Alexander, R. H. "Ezekiel." In *The Expositor's Bible Commentary: With the New International Version: Vol. 6. Isaiah, Jeremiah, Lamentations, Ezekiel,* edited by F. E. Gaebelein. Grand Rapids, Michigan: Zondervan, 1986.

Cobb, C. *"An Analysis of the Extent Christian Schools and their Bible Teachers Influence the Biblical Literacy of High School Students."* EdD diss., Southeastern Baptist Theological Seminary, 2014. Retrieved from ProQuest Dissertations and Theses.

Dick, W. O., L. Carey, and J. O. Carey. *The Systematic Design of Instruction.* 7th ed. Englewood Cliffs, New Jersey: Merrill, 2011.

Mager, R. F. *Preparing Instructional Objectives: A Critical Tool in the Development of Effective Instruction.* 3rd ed. Atlanta, Georgia: Center for Effective Performance, 1997.

Ledford, B. R., and P. J. Sleeman. *Instructional Design: System Strategies.* Greenwich, Connecticut: IAP, 2002.

Robinson, H. *Biblical Preaching: The Development and Delivery of Expository Messages.* 2nd ed. Grand Rapids, Michigan: Baker Academic, 2001.

Rothwell, W. J., and H. C. Kazanas. *Mastering the Instructional Design Process: A Systematic Approach.* San Francisco, California: John Wiley and Sons, 2011.

Smith, P. L., and T. J. Ragan. *Instructional Design.* 3rd ed. Upper Saddle River, New Jersey: Wiley & Sons, Inc., 2005.

Schultz, T., and J. Schultz. *Why Nobody Learns Much of Anything at Church: And How to Fix it.* Loveland, Colorado: Group Publishing, 1993.

PART I

INSTRUCTIONAL ANALYSIS

Objectives for Chapters 2-5

By the end of this section, you will be able to:

- Implement a plan for gaining insight into your target audience's learning profiles.
- Utilize your specific learning environment to better support your students' learning experience.
- Perform a needs assessment to determine the essential topics that should be covered in your specific educational ministry.
- State the "Big Ideas" of your chosen topic.
- Write educational goals that will connect with your students and set the tone for summative assessments.
- Decide what steps students will need to take in order to accomplish each educational goal.

Many Christian educators start backwards when it comes to preparing biblical lessons or messages. They begin by jumping straight into the biblical text (or commentaries about the biblical text) instead of first surveying the characteristics and needs of their learners, the learning context itself, the requisite educational goals, and the scope and sequence of the content. Part I of this book (chapters 2–5) will address these areas and examine how you can incorporate them in your educational ministry context. This stage of preparation is often referred to as instructional analysis or front-end analysis. It is also what I call the macro level of developing units of instruction. Before ever considering what individual lessons will look like (the micro level), we must understand the framework that undergirds them. I want to challenge you to avoid skipping over this aspect of preparation just because it is seemingly time-consuming. In fact, you may find that performing each step now will save you time and frustration in the end. This is where the rubber meets the road, where the journey begins. So let's get started!

ANALYZE THE LEARNERS AND LEARNING ENVIRONMENT

A careful consideration of the general characteristics of the target audience may be what elevates a mundane segment of instruction into compelling, imaginative, and memorable instruction.

—Patricia Smith and Tillman Ragan

Teach them his decrees and instructions, and show them the way they are to live and how they are to behave.

—Exodus 18:20 (NIV)

In his book, *The Cross and the Switchblade*, David Wilkerson (1963) describes how he began a ministry to young gang members in New York City. Being a pastor from a small mountain church in Philipsburg, Pennsylvania, he didn't know much about gangs or even the city in which he was about to minister. However, after seeing a picture in a magazine of several young gang members accused of murder, David felt God tugging on his heart to go and reach out to them. So he drove to New York and entered the courthouse on the day of their trial. David figured that the only way he could be granted access to those young men was through the judge, so on one particular day, he tried to approach him after court had adjourned. However, David quickly found himself in the hands of police officers that swiftly escorted him out of the building. After all, it was a high-profile case and they had to follow a safety protocol. The commotion caught the attention of the press in attendance, and his name and picture ended up being broadcast through several media outlets.

He later recognized that this embarrassing incident was actually the providence of God, as it opened a door for him to speak with other troubled youth. Walking along the streets of New York, several gang members recognized him and asked him, "Aren't you the preacher they kicked out of the Michael Farmer trial?" They went on to inquire about why he was so interested in the trial, and he replied that he was simply concerned about helping teenagers, especially those in gangs. After conversing with them for several minutes, David was invited to meet some of the other members in the basement of a building not too far away. Once they arrived at the location, the gang offered him an opportunity to share a biblical message right then and there. So he spoke with all of them about the simple fact that they were loved. He told them that God understood what they were looking for when they drank and played with sex. In fact, God was yearning for them to have what they were in search of: stimulation, exhilaration, and a sense of being sought after. However, this wouldn't come from a bottle of alcohol in a cold basement. God had much bigger plans for them. At one point he paused, and someone shouted out, "Keep it up, preach. You're coming through." As he spent time with them, he began to understand just how bored, lonely, and angry they really were. He surmised, "They craved excitement, and they took it where they could find it. They craved companionship, and they took that where they could find it" (p. 45). He may not have realized it at the time, but this was the beginning of a fruitful ministry with those young people. It all began by getting to know who they were and what they genuinely needed to hear.

Whether it's in New York City, London, Denver, or New Delhi, context will always be an important consideration for any educational or ministerial setting. That is why I believe the first step we should take in designing a unit or course is getting to know our learners and the learning environment. Some may ask: Why start here? Why not begin with considering topics for our instruction? Well, the first phase of instructional design, according to Mager (1984), is figuring out where we are going through our instruction, but I don't think we can realize this until we first know who is coming with us. Many Christian educators focus their lessons on the content of the curriculum rather than first considering their audience. This is tempting because our message is the gospel of Jesus Christ, and there is nothing of greater importance in this life. However, God gives us specific audiences and contexts that we must first take into consideration. Part of the challenge in this is to not design lessons for the learners we hope to have, but rather plan for those who are right in front of us.

This is something that I believe the apostle Paul excelled at, and we would do well to emulate. Consider Paul's journey to Athens in Acts 17. While awaiting Silas and Timothy (who were still in Berea), Paul explored Athens and took note of the prevalent religious and philosophical relics of their culture. He observed many idols and altars to foreign gods, but one stopped him dead in his tracks and stirred him to stand up in the meeting of the Areopagus and declare, "People of Athens! I see that in every way you are very religious. For as I walked around and looked carefully at your objects of worship, I even found an altar with this inscription: to an unknown god. So you are ignorant of the very thing you worship—and this is what I am going to proclaim to you" (Acts 17:22–23, NIV). What I find intriguing about this passage and its surrounding context is that it was only after observing the Jews, the God-fearing Greeks, and the Epicurean and Stoic philosophers in their culture, that Paul began to reason with them in the synagogue, the marketplace, and then the Areopagus. Paul used their specific context, understandings, and surroundings to speak truth into their lives. He understood his target audience, and he discerned how to connect with them. His experience in Athens that day shows us how important it is to take into consideration the learners and the learning context God entrusts to us.

That is why the goal for this chapter will be to explain how an analysis of your learners and the learning context can impact your teaching ministry. First, I will touch on some of the many benefits of this aspect of instructional analysis. I will then convey how to build a learning profile for those in your sphere of influence and how to utilize your learning context for the betterment your students. The last segment of this chapter will bring these concepts all together and discuss how an approach called *differentiation* will allow you to incorporate the many differences that are represented in your specific educational ministry.

The Benefits of Analyzing Learners and the Learning Context

The more comprehensive the analysis is of our students and their learning contexts, the better prepared we will be to make right decisions about the instructional strategies we incorporate in our instruction. For example, having a better understanding of our students will help us determine the speed or pace of our lessons and the techniques we will use for gaining and focusing their attention. Additionally, we will know the amount of structure and organization that will be needed in the learning environment. This may include how we group students together or how we incorporate appropriate content, terminology, and even different forms of media (Smith and Ragan, 2005).

Powell and Kusuma-Powell (2011) expound on this concept by proposing four benefits that teachers reap as they learn pertinent information about their students and the learning context. First of all, the authors indicate that by considering these elements, teachers will be creating a psychologically safe environment for every learner. This involves making sure a student's need for affection, belonging, and self-esteem is met. Effective teachers not only develop rapport and trust between themselves and their students but also among the students themselves. Do students feel that your learning environment is a safe place for them to open up and be vulnerable? Will others in the class make fun of them or belittle them in some way? Trust and acceptance will break down potential barriers to learning and create a psychologically safe atmosphere where individuals can feel free to take educational risks.

Secondly, teachers will be able to identify multiple access points to the curriculum to increase engagement and success. These access points involve the connections that make the content and concepts relevant to learners. This could be through sharing similar experiences or interests, or by tapping into their way of thinking. Ledford and Sleeman (2002) add that if a learner cannot see the value or relevance to what is being taught and is unable to accept the rationale and logic behind it, then he or she will almost certainly forget what has been learned as soon as it is no longer needed for that class. This is especially important for Christian educators to understand because their students must be able to see how biblical concepts apply to their lives.

As I mentioned in the introduction of this book, my doctoral dissertation elaborated on the biblical literacy of students in Christian high schools. Part of my research study involved giving students a biblical literacy test. Most of the questions were multiple-choice, but at the end of the test, there were several fill-in-the-blank questions. One student's blunt answer to a question caught my eye as I graded it. He stated, "I don't see how this would affect a Christian's life or relationship with Christ." I have a feeling that this teenager is not alone. There are individuals in all our educational ministries who need us to help them connect the dots so they can see the relevance of what we are teaching them.

A third advantage that accompanies a teacher's knowledge of his or her students is increased emotional intelligence. **Emotional intelligence** involves our capacity to recognize our own emotions (as well as the emotions of those around us) and handle them or express them in healthy ways. Powell and Kusuma-Powell (2011) note that this often manifests in a learning environment through a teacher's empathy, patience, and ability to balance student responsibility and teacher responsibility. When teachers develop emotional intelligence, they suspend negative judgments. Instead, they learn to identify the causes of student success or failure. These causes may be outside his or her control (i.e., the complexity of the subject according to his or her intelligence). When students have trouble understanding a concept, they tend to develop a *learned helplessness*. This means they believe the difficulties cannot be overcome, and so the best thing to do is stop wasting any more time on the subject. This idea becomes fixed in their minds, and they simply stop trying. Emotionally intelligent teachers will refrain from judging the individual and will also help him or her come up with a plan that will lead to educational achievements.

Lastly, a fourth benefit of analyzing learners and their context that Powell and Kusuma-Powell describe involves **student readiness**. Teachers need to have insight into what their students are already bringing to the table. This includes the knowledge, understandings, and abilities students have in relation to the content. If some students are not ready for certain concepts, instructors will have to spend time at the beginning of the unit filling in background knowledge. Otherwise, more complex problems will inevitably end up going over students' heads. As Gunter, Estes, and Mintz (2007) point out, prior learning is the foundation for all instruction. This means that new learning should be built on prior learning, and it is why colleges don't allow individuals to take certain courses without having the proper prerequisites completed. One cannot take calculus without first being able to perform well in algebra.

Jesus understood the importance of student readiness. In John 15–16, Jesus is seen teaching his disciples and preparing them for his imminent departure and the coming of the Holy Spirit. In John 16:12 (NIV) Jesus states, "I have much more to say to you, more than you can now bear." Richards and Bredfeldt (1998) note that this passage demonstrates how much Jesus cared about his disciples' needs and readiness. He let these determine what was to be taught and how it was to be taught.

Before I move on, I think I would be remiss if I failed to mention that it is important to consider where a student's readiness or prior learning has come from. Some of your students may have formed their theological or biblical convictions based on good or bad influences, some accurate and some inaccurate. They will bring to the table all they have heard in church, Sunday school, Bible studies, and their own private reading of the Bible. In John 5:37–39, Jesus rebuked the Pharisees because they thought they completely understood the Old Testament scriptures. However, he pointed out that they misunderstood God's Word because they failed to recognize that it spoke of Jesus himself.

Moreover, we must understand that prior understanding (or pre-understanding) may come from personal experiences, cultural influences, or ethnic backgrounds. In their book, *Grasping God's Word*, Duvall and Hays (2001) admit that Christians can fall prey to what they refer to as biblical nearsightedness. This is when people read the Bible in light of their immediate circumstances instead of the circumstances of those who originally heard it or read it. We are all susceptible to this. This is why it is always important to remind our students (and ourselves) to submit to God and read the Bible humbly and be willing to lay down our attitudes and pride that we already know it all. Pre-understanding is not in itself bad, but it can lead us astray if we are not careful. Our pre-understandings should be open to change when the biblical text demands it.

The Arena of Learning Profiles

Many Christian educators fail to properly analyze the characteristics and needs of their students because they view this process as either too mundane or too time-consuming. Not only are these poor excuses, but they are also far from the truth. I have always found this undertaking interesting and rewarding because I know I am gaining insights into my students that I would not have had otherwise. Moreover, we can always find ways to become more creative and more efficient with our approach. Consider the examples listed below as they can help you in your pursuit of building learning profiles for your educational ministry.

First of all, as Smith and Ragan (2005) recommend, think about interviewing other teachers or trainers who have worked with your learners before. They may be able to give you insight into student habits or learning abilities. You may also find it beneficial to observe the members of your class to see what they are interested in, how they dress, how they communicate, etc. This may help you discern if they are the kind of individuals who are always on time or usually late, or if they are introverted or extroverted, or if they are fairly organized or moderately cluttered. Another easy way to gain information about your target population is to read books and/or articles about particular age groups and development levels that will provide general information about their interests and social development. However, keep in mind that not everything can be found in a book. You may also want to have your students complete surveys that will provide information about their backgrounds, interests, and preferred instructional delivery methods as the first class begins. This will be especially beneficial if you are unfamiliar with a particular class. The hardest part of this process will be to avoid stereotyping about certain groups or populations. Remember that they are individuals, not just clusters of people.

As you gain information about your target audience, you should be able to develop a general **learning profile** of all your students that includes information about these five areas: their general characteristics (i.e., age, gender, and cultural background), their interests, their learning style(s), their intelligence preference(s), and their spiritual maturity. (See figure 2 below.) Below is a description of these along with practical applications for each.

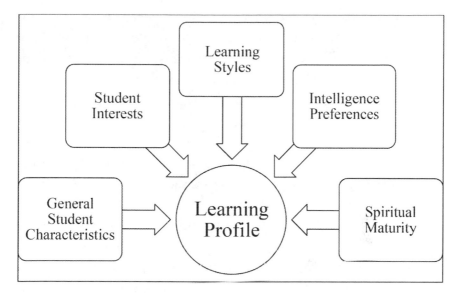

Figure 2: Elements of Learning Profiles

General Student Characteristics

The first aspect of a learning profile will involve your students' general characteristics. This includes each student's age, gender, and cultural background, as you examine how these may affect the overall learning experience. First of all, what age group are you working with? Whether you are teaching adults or children, you will still need to consider their spiritual needs, as well as their cognitive and social needs. Moreover, you should find ways to ascertain their communication skills. This will help you understand how they may relate to others in your educational ministry context and how they may react to the course content, either verbally or in written form. Also important is your student's information skills. This includes their capacity to process new information or assimilate new ideas.

Next, you will need to determine if your class will include a mix of men and women, or if it will be gender specific. Sometimes, it is helpful to split the men and women so you can discuss topics relevant to each gender. Many Christian education programs today offer these types of classes or small groups for this reason, but that is not always ideal. You will have to discern what is best for your context. Furthermore, if you do choose to have co-ed classes, keep in mind that males and females do not necessarily learn in the same way. For instance, studies show that men usually excel more at motor skills (actions) while women are more efficient at integrating analysis and intuitive thinking (perception). Additionally, women on average have better verbal memory and social cognition than men do (Lewis, 2013). So it may be beneficial in these cases to utilize teaching strategies that reflect a range of gender-based preferences (Tomlinson and Imbeau, 2010).

A third general characteristic of your students will be their cultural background. Again, Tomlinson and Imbeau propose that it is important to recognize that our students' approaches to learning may be shaped by the context in which the individual lives and by the unique ways in which people in that context make sense of and live their lives. Culture may affect how people communicate, relate to, or show respect for one another. If different cultures are represented in your educational ministry context, consider studying the diverse cultures of your students so you can have a better understanding of the relationships between culture and learning. In doing so, you will also become prepared to incorporate inclusive language in your lessons and utilize illustrations that are diverse in nature.

Student Interests

The second facet of a learning profile encompasses student interests. As mentioned earlier, teachers must ensure that their selected topics are relevant to students. Relevant topics help grab their attention. However, it is not enough to merely gain attention; teachers must learn to keep their students engaged by relating topics to student interests. Student interests involve the issues learners are concerned about, the activities they are involved in, and things that matter most to them. Getting to know the interests of your students is important as these are linked to their strengths, cultural context, personal experiences, and even their sense of need (Tomlinson and

Imbeau, 2010). Teachers increase a student's motivation to learn when they draw links between the information in the curriculum and the issues students are interested in.

Hidi and Harackiewicz (2000) argue that there are actually two types of student interest: individual interest and situational interest. Individual interest is described as a student's personal disposition to a particular topic that has developed over time. In other words, some topics will inevitably be more interesting to some students than others based on their feelings about it. For instance, some students will already be interested in discussing Eschatology because they want to know about the end times. Situational interest, on the other hand, is fostered by certain conditions and/or stimuli that focus one's attention on a certain topic. This materializes when teachers promote interest in a particular content area by modifying existing teaching materials and strategies.

In recent years, researchers have sought to determine the extent in which student engagement increases when teachers incorporate student interests in non-preferred academic areas. For example, Hinton and Kern (1999) observed a number of middle school students in an effort to see if incorporating student interests in assignments would help ensure students would complete their homework. Their baseline students only completed about 60% of their homework assignments. However, after incorporating student interests in the assignments, homework completion improved to over 95%. This study, among others, shows us how valuable incorporating student interests can be.

A great way to incorporate student interests is by using metaphors in lessons or assignments. I've heard it said that metaphors are the key to lasting communication. These figures of speech or word pictures cause students to use their imaginations, and they form lasting connections between what matters to them and the points we are trying to make. Jesus masterfully drew inferences about theological matters through the use of parables that involved his disciples' interests (e.g., sowing, harvesting, fishing). We should follow his example and incorporate metaphors in our lessons that link our students' interests with the content we teach. This will make our lessons more personally relevant for students.

Learning Styles

Knowledge of your students' **learning styles** and preferred ways of learning comprises the third piece of a learning profile. According to Bernice and Dennis McCarthy (2006), a student's learning style involves how he or she perceives or receives information and then processes that information. In your educational ministry, have you ever noticed that some students are eager to jump in and try something new while others merely watch what is happening and then reflect on it? This often occurs because students have differing learning styles. As LeFever (2004) explains, "Each person's individual learning style is as unique as a signature. When a person has something difficult to learn, that student learns faster and enjoys learning more if his or her unique learning style is affirmed by the way the teacher teaches" (p. 17). LeFever goes on to argue that students who are allowed to function in their own unique learning styles will be challenged to tackle the implications of the material, and they will be inspired to put into practice what they have learned.

Based on the detection of four distinct learning styles, Bernice McCarthy (1990) developed an approach to lesson planning called the "4MAT System." This method of delivery will be discussed further in a later chapter, but for the purposes of this section, it is important to understand the author's designation of four distinct styles of learning (based on David Kolb's research). First of all, she explains that some students in your class will be *imaginative learners*. Imaginative learners want to be personally involved in their education and discern the "big picture" that is portrayed in their classes. They desire to make connections within the content and see the relevance of what they are learning. Their favorite part of your lesson will be when you explain the "why" behind what you are teaching. Moreover, they will probably enjoy talking in class and sharing their life experiences, as they learn through their feelings and observations.

Secondly, McCarthy indicates that some students in your classes can be characterized as *analytic learners*. These individuals are more structured and want to learn new facts or concepts in each lesson. Lectures are a great way to reach analytic learners, as they look to the teacher to be the primary information giver. They sit and assess what is being presented, and they wait to see all the data before making an informed decision on how to handle it. Thirdly, *common sense learners* like to make sense of what is learned. They are the hands-on learners in your class that like to experiment or test a hypothesis. If something works, then they will use it. They will do their best when given the opportunity to deal with the parts of the content that are practical and important to them. Lastly, the fourth of McCarthy's learning styles involves *dynamic learners*. These learners like to find creative ways to use the information given in class. They are the risk takers, the entrepreneurs, the ones who thrive on flexibility and change. They learn best through trial and error (McCarthy, 1990; LeFever, 2004).

In the book, *Christian Education: Foundations for the Future*, Marlene LeFever (1991) emphasizes three additional types of learning styles that teachers should keep in mind: auditory, visual, and tactical/kinesthetic. Auditory learners prefer to learn by listening to lectures. Some may even record a lesson and listen to it all over again later just to help them learn the material better. These students often learn very well in groups and benefit more from cooperative learning. Visual learners, on the other hand, need to see what they are learning. These learners look to PowerPoint presentations, pictures, or movie illustrations to give them visual representations of what they are learning. Visual learners also enjoy taking notes, drawing diagrams, or creating charts as part of their lessons. LeFever reports that visual learners score twenty to twenty-five percent less on tests when they are taught any other way. They need to see the words or pictures in order to learn. Lastly, tactical/kinesthetic learners prefer to learn with their hands by manipulating resources. They may not like to take notes in class, but they may want to type them up or color-code them later. These learners require movement; objects they can touch, feel, or manipulate. Teachers can reach out to their tactical/ kinesthetic learners by incorporating class projects, simulations, or service projects that get them involved.

LeFever also points out that most people are mixes of different learning styles, but an individual will usually have one that is predominant. So do your best to find out what that is for each of your students, and challenge yourself to look for ways to involve the strengths of each style in every class you teach. With that said, I do believe that you should give room for them to stretch and grow in other areas as well. This is important because in the real world, they will not always have the luxury of being in their ideal situation.

You may also want to keep in mind that the students in your class may also have preferred ways of learning. These are not learning styles per se, but instead habits or behaviors that students often employ to help them absorb the information. Below are several examples of these for you to consider.

- Some students enjoy working alone, while others work best with partners.
- Some need a quiet place to study, while others prefer to listen to music while working.
- Some desire a bright room to work in, while others prefer a dark room.
- Some say that warmer class temperatures help them remain focused, while others prefer cooler temperatures.
- Some sit still and learn, while others learn best when they are on the move.
- Some enjoy being at a desk, while others like to lie down on a couch.

Intelligence Preferences

The fourth feature of a learning profile incorporates student intelligence preferences. Before I go on, let me quickly mention that some people confuse intelligence preference and learning styles, but they are indeed unique in their own respects. As explained above, learning styles involve how a student perceives or receives information and then processes that information. However, an **intelligence preference** deals with the different intellectual abilities or hardwired aptitudes students have for learning or thinking. This involves their actual ability to learn.

Before the time of Howard Gardner, it was believed that there was a singular form of intelligence, and it was determined by the intelligence quotient (IQ) test. However, Gardner discovered that this IQ test only measured two types of intelligence (one's logical-mathematical and linguistic abilities). In his book, *Frames of Mind: The Theory of Multiple Intelligences*, Garder (1983) postulated that humans possess many other types of intelligence as well. He saw the potential of the human brain as it contains different "frames of mind" or intellectual competences that lead to greater learning in each individual. He originally proposed seven different kinds of human intelligence but has since incorporated an eighth and possibly a ninth (Gardner, 1999, 2011). Each type of intelligence is determined by a combination of one's biology and cultural influences. They are listed below.

- *Linguistic intelligence.* This type of intelligence involves the ability to master language. Linguistic learners enjoy manipulating words to express them more creatively or poetically. They possess oral and communication skills.
- *Logical-mathematical intelligence.* This encompasses one's ability to see patterns, reason deductively, and think logically. Most often, this is related to scientific and mathematical thinking. They understand numbers and logical concepts.
- *Musical intelligence.* This involves a heightened ability to recognize and compose musical tones and rhythms. Obviously, musicians would be included in this group.
- *Spatial intelligence.* This engages one's ability to create mental images to solve problems. They can differentiate

between lines, shapes, and space. Applications of this kind of intelligence would be sculpting or map designing.

- *Bodily-kinesthetic intelligence.* This revolves around the ability of a person to coordinate his or her own bodily movements. Athletes are great examples of those attuned with this aptitude as are often more flexible, coordinated, and balanced.
- *Interpersonal intelligence.* The ability to see the feelings and intentions of others. Some people are more gifted at discerning the motivations or moods of others.
- *Intrapersonal intelligence.* The ability to understand one's own feelings and motivations and to be able to use that information to improve his or her own life. Individuals who grapple with their strengths and weaknesses are encamped in this intelligence.
- *Naturalist intelligence.* Those who possess a greater ability to gather data about the natural world fall into this category. They categorize new species and analyze organisms.

Kathy Koch (2007) suggests that to better understand Gardner's multiple intelligences, one can present more user-friendly labels (as she adapted them from Tom Armstrong).

- Word smart = Linguistic intelligence
- Logic smart = Logical-mathematical intelligence
- Music smart = Musical intelligence
- Picture smart = Spatial intelligence
- Body smart = Bodily-kinesthetic intelligence
- People smart = Interpersonal intelligence
- Self smart = Intrapersonal intelligence
- Nature smart = Naturalistic intelligence

McGee and Hantla (2012) discuss how multiple intelligences align with Scripture. They reason that we can find inferences in Scripture that seem to communicate different types of intelligences. For example, in Genesis 4, we learn that Cain's descendants were gifted in composing music (musical intelligence). They also forged metal objects (possessing spatial and bodily-kinesthetic intelligences). Then in Genesis 6, it can be seen that Noah and his sons possessed a certain ability to build an ark (requiring spatial, bodily-kinesthetic, mathematical-logical intelligences). A third example can be seen in Exodus 36 where we are informed that God gifted Bezalel and Oholiab for the construction of the tabernacle (necessitating spatial, bodily-kinesthetic, mathematical-logical, interpersonal, intrapersonal, and linguistic intelligences).

The implication of multiple intelligences for educational ministry is for teachers to structure the presentation of the material (and the assignments given in conjunction with the material) in a way that will lend itself to multiple intelligence preferences. Let me give you an example of how I do this in my classes. For a systematic theology course that I teach in churches and Christian schools, I give students a project involving the attributes of God (I actually received the idea for this project from a teaching teammate of mine). After teaching through the attributes of God, the ensuing assignment requires students to create an artistic project to illustrate an attribute of God. Students can write a story or a poem based on the content (word smart), draw a picture/make a painting or make a collage representing what was learned (picture smart), write a song about involving the content (music smart), acquire a photograph from nature that was inspired by something learned (nature smart), create a dance that describes the physical reactions one had in response to the content (body smart), or anything else they could come up with creatively. In other words, they can use their preferred intelligence. Students can work together on this project (people smart), but everyone is required to write an individual essay that accompanies it (self smart and/or logic smart). This essay will not only describe how the project ties into what was learned, but it will also include some self-reflection about the process and future applications. Every time I teach this class, it becomes a favorite project for the students (even with my adult classes in church). I'm always pleasantly surprised by the time and creativity they all put into the project.

Spiritual Maturity

Lastly, as a Christian educator, your learning profile should include a description of the spiritual maturity of your students. As with learning styles and intelligence preferences, there will inevitably be a number of students in your class who exhibit various levels of spiritual maturity. The more information you have about the spiritual lives of your students, the better suited you will be to share appropriate material with them. For instance, some of the students in your class may not yet be Christians. If this is the case, spend time in your classes defending the authority of the Bible, as well as explaining God's plan of salvation through the Old and New Testaments. Have one-on-one conversations with them before and after class, and do your best to answer their questions when they arise. If you are in a church setting, it may be helpful to start a class specifically for individuals who have serious questions about the faith. This may even provide an open door for congregational members to invite friends to church who are unbelievers.

Other students in your classes may be new believers who have just recently become more acquainted with the Bible. In her book, *Understanding Spiritual Maturity*, Cynthia White (2007) writes that new believers often have a great love and zeal for the Lord; they are excited about joining God's family. However, they are lacking in biblical knowledge because they have not had the opportunity to develop the skills needed to study God's Word. Stanbrough (2000) adds that new believers should be afforded the opportunity to come and know the basics about the Trinity, the Bible, sin, the world, Satan, and the Christian life (e.g., love, mercy, grace, stewardship, fellowship, forgiveness). So don't feel that you have to rush to teach them deep theological concepts. Think about it this way: If you have little children, do you attempt to teach them everything there is to know about life or do you wait to discuss certain topics until they are at the appropriate age? Similarly, you don't have to explain harder concepts to new believers right out of the gate. Spiritual growth takes time; no one becomes a mature believer overnight. So become a spiritual mentor for new believers in and out of your educational ministry context. Lead and guide them as they begin their journey towards Christlikeness.

Unfortunately, not all believers mature as quickly as we would like. There may be some individuals who enter your class who have been saved for many years, yet are still acting like infants when it comes to their spiritual maturity. This may be due to a certain sin that has taken root in their lives. Or perhaps some individuals in your class have had questions about God for many years that have gone unanswered, and so they are unsure about certain aspects of the faith. Others may have gone through a tragedy in their lives and have been questioning whether or not God really cares about their struggles. Whatever the reason for their stunted growth, our goal as Christian educators should be to reach out and help them reestablish their faith.

A fourth group of students that you may encounter in your class will be those who have become more mature in their faith. These believers need to be challenged to continue to grow in Christ and learn how to become responsible for their own continued spiritual growth. Additionally, they need to be taught how to live intentionally and choose service for the kingdom of God. More mature believers should be equipped with the tools necessary to teach others about the truths of Scripture.

In the book of Ephesians, Paul states that ministry leaders are given to the church by Christ to equip the saints for works of service and build them up into maturity. In Ephesians 4:14–15 (NIV), he goes on to say that once we as believers become mature, "Then we will no longer be infants, tossed back and forth by the waves, and blown here and there by every wind of teaching and by the cunning and craftiness of people in their deceitful scheming. Instead, speaking the truth in love, we will grow to become in every respect the mature body of him who is the head, that is, Christ." So as you evaluate your learners, think about where they are on their journey towards Christlikeness. Consider the following questions (adapted from Stanbrough, 2000) as you attempt to discern their spiritual maturity.

- How committed and serious are they about their relationships to Christ?
- Are they vitally interested in and immersed in reading and studying the Word of God?
- What sort of prayer life do they have?
- What kind of an environment are they in-are their families and communities conducive to reinforcement of spiritual things, or not?
- What kind of mentoring do they already have-lots of dedicated Christians and church support, or not?

The Influence of the Learning Environment

The **learning environment** (also referred to as the learning context) can be described as the physical and emotional context in which learning occurs (Tomlinson and Imbeau, 2010). These two important elements need to be well thought out. The first includes the physical arrangement and characteristics of the area where learning will occur. The learning environment should be flexible and support student access to a variety of learning options. Michael S. Lawson in Clark, Johnson, and Sloat (1991) proposes that several questions should guide the development of the physical learning environment.

- Which elements in my setting can I control?
- Are these assisting in the learning experience?
- What can I do to improve the educational ministry setting?

Within the physical environment, lighting can be an issue or an asset. Teachers need to ensure there is enough light for instructional tasks (e.g., reading biblical passages, taking notes, working in groups). However, they also need to make sure they are able to dim the lights for viewing presentations or videos. Additionally, consider the temperature of your learning space. A room that is too hot or too cold can delimit one's ability to concentrate. If you want students to work in groups, you will also need to make sure your space will allow it.

Lawson suggests that aesthetics is also an important factor as room decorations, posters, banners, or visual reminders can reinforce a lesson or theme.

In the book, *Mapping Out Curriculum in Your Church: Cartography for Christian Pilgrims*, Karen Estep (2012) states that a consideration of a room's physical environment will also include the materials and resources available to both teachers and their learners. When it comes to the furniture and space in your class, does it allow for the learning activities that you are planning? This includes aspects of your class like the seating arrangement. Johnson and Johnson (2009) submit that seating arrangements are often disregarded in many classes. However, the way in which students sit in relation to one another will influence their attentiveness and participation. When students have easy eye contact with others in the class, it will enhance their interaction, friendliness, and cooperativeness. On the other hand, more formal seating arrangements tend to make students feel more anxious and withdrawn. Another consideration when it comes to the physical environment of your class is the resources you will need in order to support learning. Estep (2012) suggests that these can refer to items that can be purchased, collected, or printed (e.g., educational games, craft materials, writing utensils, or printed curriculum resources). For example, you will need to check if your room will have internet access if your instruction requires online videos or presentations. If those videos require sound or a projector, then make sure that there is appropriate equipment in working order. If you will use class handout notes, then you will need a working printer and copier.

The second aspect of the learning environment that is often overlooked involves the emotional context. This has to do with the culture of your educational ministry context. Students will learn best when they feel safe, respected, involved, challenged, and supported. You may need to think about whether you will have a more open and flexible environment or more of a structured one. Either way, make sure that, as the teacher, you are able to promote respect and support the possibilities that are in each student. Along with this, encourage your students to learn to respect and support each other as well. In this, make sure that even in disagreements, students are still respectful of others' opinions. This is especially important when discussing debatable theological topics.

Accommodating Student Differences

Every student is different and brings his or her own personality, background, interests, learning styles, intelligence preferences, and spiritual maturity to the learning environment. Moreover, students enter each course of learning at various starting points, and they work at different speeds and process information in a variety of ways. That is why it would be beneficial to utilize the concept of differentiation in your educational ministry context. **Differentiation**, according to Tomlinson and Imbeau (2010), is an approach to teaching that considers the needs of every individual in a class. It comes from the conviction that every student is unique and important as a learner and as a human being. This truth should lead teachers to act in ways that show value to each student when it comes to making decisions about student groupings, discipline, grading, and instruction.

Effective teachers design lessons with student differences in mind by constructing a proactive plan of instruction that ensures everyone has the best possible opportunity to learn the essential knowledge or skills that are needed for a particular course. In essence, every individual will be afforded the opportunity to master and move beyond the content. This plan of instruction will differentiate the content (that which is taught), the process (the sequence and instructional methods used), and the product (what students know by the end of the course) of education for each student. For instance, teachers can offer an assortment of ways for students to receive the course material, or give alternative assessments to students who need them the most. While each lesson may be written or developed for the entire class, each individual will be able to understand it in his or her own way.

Usually, the question in this process is not if a teacher can recognize the differences that exist, but rather how he or she will be able to meet the distinctive needs of students in an environment that is comprised of so many individuals. That is why Tomlinson and Imbeau, along with Smith and Ragan (2005), suggest that teachers should accommodate student differences by creating instructional treatments, each adjusted to a narrowed range of characteristics (tracks for higher and lower achieving students). For example, when it comes to advanced learners, teachers should try to maximize interest areas. When an area particularly intrigues a certain student, he or she can be challenged to learn as much about that subject or concept as possible. If a student finishes one project early, suggest that he or she work on another subject that is particularly interesting or dig deeper on the current assignment. Another idea is to give advanced students a complex application of a certain concept they are familiar with. This allows them to use a certain concept or skill in an unfamiliar way. For example, consider giving them a reading assignment on a certain concept, then ask them to apply it to their lives in a way they never have before.

On the other hand, for lower achieving students, Tomlinson and Imbeau suggest developing learning contracts. These are designed to help teachers provide varied work for students in a focused area. To do this, a teacher will work individually with a struggling student and come up with a contract that works well. The contract should include options for the student to complete assignments with consequences for not getting the work submitted on time. Another similar idea is to offer alternative assignments. This will help eliminate a student's frustration and confusion and instead make them feel empowered by something that will help them become successful. The important thing is to give a struggling student an assignment that helps him or her make progress with past learning gaps.

Conclusion

Mark Twain is credited with this famous expression: "I can teach anybody how to get what they want out of life. The problem is that I can't find anybody who can tell me what they want." This is a challenge that, as Christian educators, we face on a regular basis. We want to make an impact in our student's lives, but to do so we must understand their characteristics and needs. That's not usually something that is common knowledge; it will take intentional effort on our part as teachers. Howard Hendricks once stated that the way people learn will determine how you teach. This means that effective teachers must understand not only the content they are teaching but also the people they are teaching it to (Hendricks, 1987).

Keeping this in mind, we must design our lessons and units to suit the learning profiles of our students. We can't structure according to our own learning styles (even though that is our natural tendency). The people around us do not necessarily learn the way we learn. As Smith and Ragan (2005) explain, we need to be aware of our tendency to explain things the way we would understand them or use examples that would be familiar to us instead of ones that would impact our target audience. Moreover, we can't assume that all learners will learn optimally under the same conditions (Ledford and Sleeman, 2002). Don't make the mistake of assuming that all your learners will learn in the same way; everyone is different. That is why we need an instructional analysis. We need to know who our learners are, how they learn the best, and we need to know what context our lessons will be taught under before even coming up with our content.

Let me close this chapter with the words of the apostle Paul from 1 Corinthians 9:19–22 (NIV).

> I have made myself a slave to everyone, to win as many as possible. To the Jews I became like a Jew, to win the Jews. To those under the law I became like one under the law (though I myself am not under the law), so as to win those under the law. To those not

having the law I became like one not having the law (though I am not free from God's law but am under Christ's law), so as to win those not having the law. To the weak I became weak, to win the weak. I have become all things to all people so that by all possible means I might save some.

Here we see how intentional Paul was in adjusting his ministry to the needs of those around him so he could reach them for Christ. We see Jesus himself doing the same thing in the gospels as he was often called "a friend of tax collectors and sinners" (Matt. 11:19; Luke 7:34). These examples should challenge us to make adjustments as necessary in our educational ministries. As Tomlinson and Imbeau (2010) put it, we need to "make room" for all kinds of learners so they can succeed.

Practice Makes Perfect

Learner Profiles and Learning Environments Worksheet

Directions: Use this worksheet as a template for answering questions about your educational ministry context (e.g., small group, Bible study, classroom, sermon series, etc.).

Educational Ministry Context: _____

1.) Learning profiles

- What are the general characteristics of my students?

- What are my students' interests?

- What are my students' learning styles?

- What types of intelligences do my students prefer?

• What is the level of my students' spiritual maturity?

2.) Learning environment

• Which elements in my educational ministry's setting can I control?

• Do existing elements assist in the learning experience?

• What can I do to improve the educational ministry setting?

• How can I describe my educational ministry's culture?

Sources

Armstrong, T. *7 Kinds of Smarts: Identifying and Developing Your Multiple Intelligences.* New York, New York: Plume, 1999.

Duvall, J. S., and J. D. Hays. *Grasping God's Word: A Hands on Approach to Reading, Interpreting, and Applying the Bible.* Grand Rapids, Michigan: Zondervan, 2001.

Estep, J., R. White, and K. Estep. *Mapping Out Curriculum in Your Church: Cartography for Christian Pilgrims.* Nashville, Tennessee: B&H Publishing, 2012.

Gardner, H. *Intelligence Reframed: Multiple Intelligences for the 21st Century.* New York, New York: Basic Books, 1999.

Gardner, H. *Frames of Mind: The Theory of Multiple Intelligences.* 3rd ed. New York, New York: Basic Books, 2011.

Gardner, H. *Frames of Mind: The Theory of Multiple Intelligences.* New York, New York: Basic Books, 1983.

Gunter, M. A., T. H. Estes, and S. L. Mintz. *Instruction: A Models Approach.* 5th ed. Boston, Massachusetts: Pearson, 2007.

Hendricks, H. *Teaching to Change Lives.* Colorado Springs, Colorado: Multnomah Books, 1987.

Hidi, S., and J. M. Harackiewicz. "Motivating the Academically Unmotivated: A Critical Issue for the 21st Century." *Review of Educational Research,* 70 (2000): 151-179.

Hinton, L. M., and L. Kern. "Increasing Homework Completion by Incorporating Student Interests." *Journal of Positive Behavior Interventions,* 1 (1999): 231-241.

Johnson, D. W., and F. P. Johnson. *Joining Together: Group Theory and Group Skills.* 10th ed. Upper Saddle River, New Jersey: Pearson, 2009.

Koch, K. *How Am I Smart?* Chicago, Illinois: Moody, 2007.

Lawson, M. S. "Managing the Classroom Experience." In *Christian Education: Foundations for the Future*, edited by R. E. Clark, L. Johnson, and A. K. Sloat, 179-192. Chicago, Illinois: Moody, 1991.

Ledford, B., and P. J. Sleeman. *Instructional Design: System Strategies.* Greenwich, Connecticut: Information Age Publishing, 2002.

LeFever, M. D. "Understanding Learning Styles." In *Christian Education: Foundations for the Future*, edited by R. E. Clark, L. Johnson, and A. K. Sloat, 333-350. Chicago, Illinois: Moody, 1991.

LeFever, M. D. *Learning Styles: Reaching Everyone God Gave You to Teach.* Colorado Springs, Colorado: David C. Cook, 2004.

Lewis, T. "How Men's Brains Are Wired Differently than Women's." *Scientific American*, December 2, 2013. Retrieved from http://www.scientificamerican.com/article/how-mens-brains-are-wired-differently-than-women/

McCarthy, B. "Using the 4MAT System to Bring Learning Styles to Schools." *Educational Leadership*, 48 (October 1990): 31-37.

McCarthy, B, and D. McCarthy. *Teaching Around the 4MAT® Cycle: Designing Instruction for Diverse Learners with Diverse Learning Styles.* Thousand Oaks, California: Corwin Press, 2006.

McGee, D., and B. Hantla. "An Intelligent Review of Multiple Intelligences: A Christian Critique of Howard Gardner's Theory of Multiple Intelligences for the Practice of Educational Church Leaders." *Journal of Biblical Perspectives in Leadership*, 4 (2012): 3–16.

Powell, W., and O. Kusuma-Powell. *How to Teach Now: Five Keys to Personalized Learning in the Global Classroom*. Alexandria, Virginia: ASCD, 2011.

Richards, L. O., and G. O. Bredfeldt. *Creative Bible Teaching*. Chicago, Illinois: Moody Bible Institute, 1998.

Smith, P. L., and T. J. Ragan. *Instructional Design*. 3rd ed. Upper Saddle River, New Jersey: Wiley & Sons, Inc., 2005.

Stanbrough, D. L. *Higher Ground: The Spiritual Maturity Levels of the Christian According to the Bible*. Victory, B.C.: Trafford Publishing, 2000.

Tomlinson, C. A., and M. B. Imbeau. *Leading and Managing a Differentiated Classroom*. Alexandria, Virginia: ASCD, 2010.

White, C. V. *Understanding Spiritual Maturity*. Columbus, Georgia. Brentwood Christian Press, 2007.

Wilkerson, D. *The Cross and the Switchblade*. Grand Rapids, MI: Chosen Books, 1963.

3

DETERMINE EXISTING EDUCATIONAL GAPS

As we come to understand the needs of people, especially the people we teach, we can become more effective in teaching the Bible. By knowing our students, we can help our students not only make more direct and specific application of Scripture to their lives, but we can also help them see the very contemporary nature of the message of the Bible.

—Lawrence Richards and Gary Bredfeldt

*Instruct the wise and they will be wiser still;
teach the righteous and they will add to their learning.*

—Proverbs 9:9 (NIV)

Not too long ago, I was asked to fill in as a church's interim youth pastor after their regular youth pastor had resigned unexpectedly. He was only there for about a year, so this would be the second youth pastor change the church experienced in a short amount of time. After accepting the position, I immediately began thinking about what I should share with the students as I began my ministry with them. I spoke with the church's leadership about what they had already been discussing, and then I surveyed the students to help me obtain a better understanding of their characteristics, interests, etc. It became clear that what they needed to hear from me was a series of messages that would communicate the concept of stability

47

in their lives. As middle and high school students, they were already experiencing many changes in their lives, and now they were dealing with another pastoral change. They needed to know that despite all the changes that were happening around them, there are some things we can count on that will never change: God's Word never changes, God's love never changes, and God's mission for the church never changes.

This is just one example of how to go about developing ideas for a series of lessons or messages. What is your approach? When you consider future topics or themes to address in your educational ministry context, what procedure do you usually employ to help you make informed decisions about what to include or exclude? Hopefully, you will begin with prayer and rely on God's direction to guide you through the process. After this, however, you may choose to follow a church or school calendar, or you may have a set curriculum that regulates the subject matter for you. Book study is another popular method that you might utilize. This involves selecting a particular book of the Bible to review or another book that speaks to a spiritual topic that is at your discretion. Maybe you are like some biblical instructors who pick their topics based on what the people who attend their meetings are interested in learning. However, this can prove to be difficult as your group's felt needs may be affected by their negative perceptions about certain topics or an inability to know which topics are available. Or perhaps you prefer to discuss a certain subject matter simply because you want to teach it. But again, this method will not assure you that the topic you select will be what students need to hear at that specific time.

Choosing topics for our students to study should involve more than just a feeling that it is God's direction. Our decisions must always rest on what we know about our students and their needs (Gunter, Estes, and Mintz, 2007). Again, we can look to the example of the apostle Paul to illustrate this point as he always sought to understand the needs of those he taught. Consider his words in 1 Corinthians 3:1–3 (NIV). "Brothers and sisters, I could not address you as people who live by the Spirit but as people who are still worldly—mere infants in Christ. I gave you milk, not solid food, for you were not yet ready for it. Indeed, you are still not ready. You are still worldly. For since there is jealousy and quarreling among you, are you not worldly? Are you not acting like mere humans?" I am sure this was not what the people of Corinth wanted to hear, but it was nonetheless what they needed to hear. Paul discerned their needs, and he taught accordingly. They were not ready for the deep things of God; they needed to repeat the basics.

Similarly, as Christian educators today, we need to determine exactly what it is that our people need to hear and in what context. We need to know if they are ready for the "meat" of God's Word or if they need to go back and cover the fundamentals. But how can we do this in our many contemporary contexts today? I believe the first step involves coming to understand the discrepancies between what should be displayed through their lives and what actually is being displayed through their lives. Once this is determined, we will know what areas need to be addressed or what pieces of our content need to be communicated at that moment in time.

In instructional design, this process is referred to as a **needs assessment** (the second aspect of instructional analysis). In his book, *Deciding What to Teach and Test: Developing, Aligning, and Leading the Curriculum*, Fenwick English (2010) describes a needs assessment as a "gap analysis" of the existing knowledge and performance of students. This analysis simply lists any gaps between desired and actual levels of student performance in a particular educational program. Stated somewhat differently, a needs assessment discerns areas in which a large number of students are experiencing difficulty in and for which they are not already receiving quality instruction. Knowing if there are gaps between what learners should be able to do and what they are currently able to do will drive the scope of your instruction. Your goal will be to determine which gaps can and should be addressed with instruction (Smith and Ragan, 2005). This process will also guide subsequent decisions pertaining to the design, implementation, and evaluation of your instruction (Watkins, Meiers, and Visser, 2012).

In this chapter, I will describe the basic steps involved in performing a needs assessment. This will help you determine what subjects need to be taught in your educational ministry context. Once you have accomplished this, you will need to ensure your selection of topics remains balanced. So I will also discuss how to spend adequate time on developing biblical/theological, leadership/equipping, and spiritual formation units of study for the overall curriculum in your educational ministry. This chapter (along with chapter 2) serves as the foundation for everything you will do with your instructional design. It is after this that you will be able to develop a main theme and educational goals as you move forward in the process.

Determining the Need for Instruction

There are three distinct steps that need to be completed in the needs assessment process that are addressed below: identify ideal characteristics of spiritual development; measure the gaps between "what you want to see" and "what you currently see"; and select and prioritize measurable gaps. Due to the complex nature of these steps, I want to encourage you to collaborate with others in this endeavor. Don't be satisfied for being a lone wolf and try to figure out what to teach alone. Consider working with a teammate or perhaps a committee. Delegate certain aspects to each member to save yourself time and energy.

Step 1: Identify Ideal Characteristics of Spiritual Development

The first step in a needs assessment is to consider the wide range of possible spiritual characteristics that you hope to see in your learners, independent of what you currently perceive to subsist. The purpose of this phase is not to place value on one spiritual characteristic over another but merely to identify the total range of relevant characteristics (Burton and Merrill, in *Instructional Design* by Briggs, Gustafson, and Tillman, eds. 1991). Below are two approaches that you can employ to establish these characteristics:

the expected student outcome approach and the biblical deficiencies approach.

The Expected Student Outcome Approach

Expected student outcomes (ESOs), sometimes referred to as desired student outcomes, are statements that articulate what students are expected to know, feel, or do at the completion of their study in a particular program (English, 2010). These statements will be very general and promote your values and mission as a church or educational institution. In the context of a church, these statements should be applicable for learners throughout their experience in every ministry or program available (e.g., youth ministry, small group ministry, Sunday school ministry, etc.). Similarly, educational institutions should generate statements that will be applicable for each department and/or age group.

It should be noted that ESOs will be a natural extension of your mission, vision, and purpose statements. These statements explain why your organization exists, what is unique about your program, and how individual ministries contribute to your overall purpose. Hopefully, your mission statements will include a section about your plan for discipleship/educational ministry. Below is an example of one of my former church's plans (The Church on the Hill in Dundee, Florida).

> We diligently seek to develop new Christians as faithful, functioning followers of Christ, while also helping established Christians mature in their spiritual journey through teaching, mentoring, and accountability (John 15:1–8; Acts 2:42; Rom. 6:1–6; Eph. 3:14–21; Col. 1:21–23; 2 Tim. 2:1–2, 15; Heb. 5:12–14; 1 Peter 2:1–3).

Given this statement (and our overall vision/mission statements), I created a number of ESOs or characteristics of spiritual growth that we desired to see depicted in the lives of church members.

- Students will grow in their knowledge and understanding of the Bible as the divinely and infallible Word of God.
- Students will be prepared to articulate and defend the gospel of Jesus Christ.
- Students will allow the renewing work of the Holy Spirit to help them become relationally healthy and emotionally healed.
- Students will make intentional effort to live out their faith through love, obedience, and service.
- Students will know how to be good stewards of their time, talents, and treasures.
- Students will commit to become spiritually mature and discover how to lead in ministry and vocation.
- Students will appreciate the importance of mentorship and accountability.

So what are your ESOs? Take some time now to focus on the areas that God has put on your heart that you want your learners to excel in. In this pursuit, you may find it useful to consider Ruth Beechick's (1981) research. She astutely transformed Robert Havighurst's work of identifying the different roles people adopt in life into spiritual development tasks that differing ages need to cultivate (Richards and Bredfeldt, 1998; Pazmino, 2008). You can align your ESOs with the spiritual development of your target audience. A summary of these tasks is given in figure 3 below. As you look at this list, what stands out to you? Are there any spiritual characteristics/tasks that you add to this list? You may perceive that there are some tasks that can be completed by numerous age groups at differing levels. Also consider which tasks would be appropriate for new believers. How would you determine what elementary truths should be taught for their spiritual context?

Spiritual Development Tasks

Preschool Age

1.) Experience love, security, discipline, joy, and worship.
2.) Beginning to develop awareness and concepts of God, Jesus, and other basic Christian realities.
3.) Developing attitudes toward God, Jesus, church, self, the Bible.
4.) Beginning to develop concepts of right and wrong.

Elementary School Years

1.) Receiving and acknowledging Jesus Christ as Savior and Lord.
2.) Growing awareness of Christian love and responsibility in relationships with others.
3.) Continuing to build concepts of basic Christian realities.
4.) Learning basic Bible teachings adequate for personal faith and everyday Christian living, including teachings in these areas: (prayer in daily life, the Bible in daily life, Christian friendships, group worship, responsibility for serving God, basic knowledge of God, Jesus, Holy Spirit, creation, angelic beings, Heaven, Hell, sin, salvation, Bible literature, and history).
5.) Developing healthy attitudes toward self.

Adolescence

1.) Learning to show Christian love in everyday life.
2.) Continuing to develop healthy attitudes toward self.
3.) Developing Bible knowledge and intellectual skills adequate for meeting intellectual assaults on faith.
4.) Achieving strength of Christian character adequate for meeting anti-Christian social pressures.
5.) Accepting responsibility for Christian service in accordance with growing abilities.
6.) Learning to make life decisions on the basic of eternal Christian values.
7.) Increasing self-discipline to "seek those things which are above."

Tasks of Maturity

1.) Accepting responsibility for one's own continued growth and learning.
2.) Accepting biblical responsibilities toward God and toward others.
3.) Living a unified, purposeful life centered upon God.

Figure 3: Ruth Beechick's Spiritual Development Tasks

The Biblical Deficiencies Approach

The second approach for identifying areas that need to be addressed in educational ministry programs is concerned with actual biblical knowledge. What components of biblical knowledge do you think are essential for all Christians to possess? If we know what these areas are, we can pinpoint where our students are lacking (or where they are deficient) and gear up our lessons to fill those gaps.

As part of his doctoral dissertation, Jeff Crawford (2002) worked with several biblical/theological scholars to determine what makes a person biblically literate. Their combined efforts resulted in the development of nine components of biblical knowledge.

1.) Salvation history
2.) Historical background of the Old and New Testaments
3.) Significant people in the Old Testament
4.) Significant people in the New Testament
5.) Significant events in the Old Testament
6.) Significant events in the New Testament
7.) Significant texts in the Old Testament
8.) Significant texts in the New Testament
9.) An understanding of the plan of salvation and the role of Jesus

Within these nine areas, the panel also recommended instruction in the areas of the creation narrative, the patriarchal period, the Exodus, the conquest of Canaan, the time of the Judges, the Hebrew monarchies, the Exile, the intertestamental period, the life of Jesus, Paul's life and letters, the differences in the different genres of the Bible, and the purpose of Scripture in determining normative faith and practice.

How exhaustive do you feel this list is? Would you add certain biblical features? If so, what would you include? Personally, I would add the importance of the priests and the shedding of sacrificial blood. I would also emphasize the Law of Moses, along with several other things. There are so many important topics in the Bible to consider. What are your non-negotionables when it comes to what you want your people to know?

Step 2: Measure the Gaps between 'What You Want to See' and 'What You Currently See'

Once you have a firm grasp on what you expect from your students, you can begin to look for and measure gaps in learning. Hopefully, you will have already completed a thorough analysis of the characteristics your students (referring back to chapter 2) and compiled your list of essential characteristics of spiritual development/biblical knowledge. Now you will determine their current performance levels (from the goals from step one) and compare the performance to the desired (what ought to be) performance level (Burton and Merrill, 1991). Put simply, measure the gaps, and see where they are lacking.

In order to do this, you will have to identify potential sources of data and establish criteria on which decisions will be made about what to do. Below, I will explain how to use five distinctive assessment tools to help you in this process (adapted for educational ministry purposes from Watkins, Meiers, and Visser, 2012). Before I share these with you, let me just give you a word of caution: be careful not to make assumptions or generalize to whole groups of people. In any group of people, there will be differing levels of knowledge gaps/ needs, but still do your best to pinpoint what your target audience needs the most.

Scenarios

The purpose of this needs assessment tool is to explore of the potential strengths and weaknesses of student performance. Scenarios can be given to the class as a whole, or on an individual basis. Teachers may choose to discuss scenarios with students in class or have them compose essays in which they are required to articulate how they would respond in a given situation. For example, teachers discussing cults with students may want to ask them, "If several

Jehovah's Witnesses knocked on your door and wanted to talk about how Jesus was coming back on December 31st, 2017, what would you say to them?" A student's response will give the teacher insight into his or her current knowledge base. This will help them determine what areas of the content need to be emphasized in class. According to Watkins, Meiers, and Visser, scenarios are most useful in situations where the number of possible directions is large or where there is a large degree of uncertainty. The key to this approach is in developing realistic scenarios for students, and then letting students grapple with how to respond. To help in this endeavor, you may want to consider building uncertainties or unexpected events into each scenario. Make each scenario more meaningful by providing varying perspectives, including positive and pessimistic views. Once the initial assessment has concluded, you will be able to identify potential solutions for the class that will reach to the causes of the problem while at the same time accomplishing desired results.

Duel-Response Surveys (Self-Assessments)

As mentioned in the introduction to this chapter, it is difficult to simply ask your learners about their felt needs (and what they want to learn) because this may be affected by their negative perceptions or their inability to know what is available. However, as Watkins, Meiers, and Visser explain, a **duel-response survey** is uniquely designed in a way that will measure their perspectives about their current and desired performance levels. This is different than traditional single-response surveys in that it specifically provides clear data regarding the size, direction, and relative priority of performance gaps. These are valuable pieces of information that will be essential to the unique goals of a needs assessment. It may be valuable to note that any survey will only measure perceptions, not performance. A person may perceive that he or she is performing high in an area, but in actuality, he or she struggles without knowing it. That is why it would be helpful to have a person fill it out for him or herself and then have a friend or spouse fill it out as well to compare notes. Either way, knowing perceptions will be essential to making informed decisions.

When creating your survey, utilize your list of ESOs or spiritual development tasks to focus questions. For example, one of Beechick's spiritual development tasks for adults is accepting responsibility for one's continued growth and learning. Create a question for this in a duel-response format using Likert-type scales (table 1 gives an example for how to do this). Consider including questions that analyze frequency (scale: 1 = daily; 2 = weekly; 3 = monthly; 4 = every few months; 5 = never), satisfaction (scale: 1 = very dissatisfied; 2 = dissatisfied; 3 = neutral; 4 = satisfied; 5 = very satisfied), or agreement questions (scale: 1 = strongly disagree; 2 = disagree; 3 = neutral; 4 = agree; 5 = strongly agree).

To evaluate the results, simply subtract the value assigned to the current column from the value assigned to the desired column. The difference between each result will identify discrepancies or gaps (the bigger the gap, the greater the need). In my example, the student's gap between accepting responsibility for growth and learning was not as wide as the gap between accepting biblical responsibilities. Of course, you should not make decisions about topics or themes based on one person's survey, so attempt to get to the heart of as many people as you can in your educational ministry. Whatever your class is struggling with the most (or whatever gaps they face the most), develop units of instruction to help them in those areas.

Instructions: Indicate your level of agreement with the survey questions below (Scale: 1=Strongly disagree; 2=Disagree; 3=Neutral; 4=Agree; 5=Strongly agree).		
Current Performance	Survey Question	Desired Performance
1 (2) 3 4 5	I accept responsibility for my continued growth and learning	1 2 3 4 (5)
1 2 (3) 4 5	I accept my biblical responcibilities toward God and others?	1 2 3 (4) 5

Table 1: Duel-Response Survey Questions

Interviews and Observations

Any research project becomes more valuable when researchers are able to talk to or observe those that they are studying. The purpose of interviews is to collect information from a single person or small groups of people that can provide a valuable in-depth context as to why a person (or people) may or may not be excelling in an area. Interviewers are able to ask for elaboration or explanation with follow-up questions that may have been limited through a survey. On the other hand, observations document how people are growing or have become stagnant in certain areas. Put together, interviews and observations help determine what is working and what is not working in the current educational process.

Before you conduct interviews or seek to observe members of your target audience, determine which ESOs or spiritual development tasks you want to evaluate. For interviews, create a series of questions based on those (and possible follow-up questions). You can even do this in the duel-response format that was explained above. Ask these questions for example: How well do you currently accept responsibility your continued growth and learning? How much do you desire for this to grow in your life? When interviewing people, always remember to listen more than you talk.

For observations, you will need to develop a list of spiritual health indicators that will convey to you whether or not your people are growing in the areas you have chosen. For example: Is there unity or disunity in your educational ministry? Can you see heartfelt motivation to follow God in your student's lives? When they are treated unfairly, how do they respond? Do they treat people with respect and value? Are they willing to help the disenfranchised, the poor, and the oppressed? How often do they witness to others, and are they effective at doing so? When they sin, are they quick to repent?

SWOT Analysis

Another practical way to assess your target audience and their needs is by conducting a SWOT analysis with a team of leaders from your educational ministry. The acronym SWOT stands for *strengths* (areas where they excel spiritually and do not require instruction at this time), *weaknesses* (areas where they are lacking spiritually and can use instruction), *opportunities* (possible biblical themes or examples that may speak to their weaknesses or make their strengths even stronger), and *threats* (possible external or internal factors that have limited their ability to grow spiritually in a certain area). What I like about this technique is that it allows groups to brainstorm together to identify gaps.

The process for conducting a SWOT analysis starts with gathering together a team of your teachers, staff, pastors, deacons, and/or elders that can speak to the needs of your target audience. Whoever you choose, make sure that they represent diversity in their perspectives. Ask each of them to pinpoint how they believe your ESOs or spiritual development tasks are being displayed in the lives of your learners. Try to come up with several strengths, weaknesses, opportunities, and threats, and place them together in a SWOT matrix (see table 2 for an example). Then build consensus within your team so that it will inform your decisions about topics that should be covered in your lessons. Also, consider the courses of study that have been recently been conducted in your educational ministry. If your learners just went through a study on identity during the last year, then they probably will not need to study that subject or similar subjects again right away.

SWOT Analysis	
ESO: Students will be prepared to articulate and defend the Gospel of Jesus Christ. *Ministry Context:* Small group Bible study on Sunday nights	
Strengths	*Weaknesses*
S1: Students completed a unit on Christian Theology this past spring.	W1: A majority of students in the class still have difficulty articulating their faith.
S2: Students completed a unit on Islam last year.	W2: A growing number of students seemingly avoid one-on-one evangelism.
S3: Students are engaged in an outreach ministry that feeds and prays for the less fortunate every month.	W3= Students have not been taught about other religious traditions and worldviews (besides Islam).
Opportunities	*Threats*
O1: Students have expressed a desire for class sessions to to be taped so they can listen to the ones that were missed (along with the handout notes).	T1= A number of students struggle to attend every session, which can lead gaps in their learning.
O2: Possible studies: Bill Hybels' book/resource "Just walk across the room," or Halverson's book "The compact guide to world religions."	T2= Communication between class members can be a challenge (in and out of class).
O3= There are some upcoming short-term mission trip and other outreach opportunities available to students in the near future.	T3: Some students have expressed a judgemental (and even critical) attitude towards individuals that adhere to other religions.

Table 2: SWOT Analysis Example

Biblical Knowledge Evaluation

This last method of measurement will quantify your target audience's knowledge of specific areas of the Bible. Use biblical literacy tests to determine where your learners are falling short and then address those areas in class. For my doctoral dissertation, I used Jeff Crawford's (2002) biblical literacy test to measure the knowledge of Christian high school students. He developed this test alongside his expert panel of biblical/theological scholars. I believe this test would be a great resource for you to use as well. With his permission, I have included it in the "Practice Makes Perfect" section at the end of this chapter.

One of the things I appreciate about this particular biblical literacy test is the fact that Crawford intentionally grouped each question according to the major component of biblical emphasis that his panel decided upon. Questions 1–9 deal with salvation history. They also involve the historical backgrounds of the New and Old Testaments. Questions 14, 19, 23, 24, 25, and 29 also deal with historical background information. Significant people from the Old Testament are found in questions 15, 17, 24, 30, 32, and 35. Significant people from the New Testament are found in questions 10, 20, 23, and 33. Events in the Old Testament that were deemed as significant are found in questions 12, 14, 21, 24, 25, 31, and 35. Events in the New Testament that were deemed as significant are found in questions 9, 11, 13, 18, 23, and 29. Texts from the Old Testament that were deemed as significant are found in questions 15, 16, 17, 18, 21, 22, and 26. Texts from the New Testament that were deemed as significant are found in questions 11, 13, 18, 20, 27, 28, and 34. Lastly, to gauge a student's understanding of the plan of salvation through Christ, you would need to look at questions 20, 23, 27, 28, and 34. Consider giving this test or another biblical literacy test to your students to assess where they are at in their knowledge of different areas of the Bible.

Step 3: Select and Prioritize Measurable Gaps

After completing the first two steps of your needs assessment, you may notice that there are a number of gaps or spiritual deficiencies that preside in your specific educational ministry. Because of this, it may be helpful to differentiate between the different types of gap results that you may discover. Watkins, Meiers, and Visser (2012) have identified three such categories. First of all, *continuing needs* include gap results that are known from previous assessments. These are monitored in an ongoing manner. Secondly, *changing needs* represent gaps in results that adjust in size, scope, or importance depending on internal or external changes in an organization or community. Thirdly, *emerging needs* signify gaps that emerge when new desired results are identified, or when there are unforeseen changes in current performance. Given these differing types of gaps, step three of the needs assessment process is meant to help you decipher which type of gap is most representative of your context and which gaps should be addressed with instruction.

Can all gaps be resolved through instruction? Not necessarily. You may recognize that those within your target audience may not be exhibiting ideal conduct because of poor situations at home, struggles with sin, depression, etc. These are not easily alleviated, even through instruction. They will require the love and support of a fellow Christian on the narrow road. Differentiate these gaps from areas that you can help remedy through instruction. Focus your attention on those areas, but do not neglect the other gaps. Make sure students get the care they need in every area of their lives.

In this process, you may also want to consider Wiggins and McTight's (2005) suggestions as to what filters you should use when deciding which gaps to tackle or topics to select. The first filter involves choosing a topic that has enduring value beyond the learning environment. These truths or understandings should be more than simply facts or skills but instead focus on concepts, principles, or processes. They should be topics that can be readily applied to daily life. Secondly, make sure your content decisions are based on what experts in the discipline believe to be core knowledge. Utilize Crawford's expert panel as mentioned above or use other sources you trust. A third filter to consider has to do with the extent that the topics need to be unpacked. Our goal as teachers should be to make abstract ideas into more connected, meaningful, and useful ideas. The authors propose asking several questions when searching for topics that need to be unpacked before they can be understood: What important concepts do students often have difficulty grasping? What do they typically struggle with? What topics involve misconceptions that need to be cleared up? Whatever those topics are, they will be worthwhile in discussing or unpacking for them. The fourth filter looks to the extent that the topic offers potential engagement for students. Consider annexing topics that are inherently interesting to students of various ages. Ask yourself if this is a topic that may seem dry on the surface but can be made alive through connecting it to student interests.

In addition to these four filters, I would also like to propose adding a fifth to this list. It comes from the writings of Lev Vygotsky, a Russian psychologist from the early twentieth century whose work has become very influential in recent years in North America. He proposed that learning should be matched to a student's **zone of proximal development**. This includes areas of learning in which students require interaction or support from others (e.g., teachers and/or peers) in order to attain expertise. As Vygotsky (1978) states, "The zone of proximal development defines those functions that have not yet matured but are in process of maturation, functions that will mature tomorrow but are currently in an embryonic state" (p. 86). This means we should concentrate on concepts or skills in which students have the potential to grasp or develop in but can't quite do it on their own yet. They require the assistance of more competent peers or teachers. This explains why apprenticeships or mentorships are so valuable in educational ministries. The implications of Vygotsky's research is that the most meaningful learning will take place when students are working on tasks that are at the right level of difficulty for them. Robert Slavin (2009) expounds on this by giving an example of an elementary math student. He states that if a certain student could not find the median of a set of numbers by him or herself, but could do it with the help of a teacher, then finding medians is probably in that student's zone of proximal development. Applying this to educational ministries, if your gap analysis discovered that students in your class were only able to correctly utilize the numbering system of a *Strong's Concordance* when you personally walked them through the process, then that skill is in their zone of proximal development. They were able to do it with your help, but they still need further instruction (and practice) to fully comprehend the skill for themselves.

Once you have selected possible topics that are worth discussing, your task is to determine which of the gaps are most critical so you can address those first. Write down each gap, based on current results and desired results, and prioritize which ones are of most importance to tackle first. Smith and Ragan (2005) give several criteria that will help you prioritize which areas you should concern yourself with first.

- The size of the gap (attend to the biggest first).
- The importance of the goal (working on the most critical are first).
- The number of students affected (choosing those gaps that affect the largest number of students).
- The consequences of not meeting the goal (select gaps that have the most serious consequences for not meeting them).
- The probability of reducing the gap (attending to the gaps that have the greatest probability of being closed).

Ensure that the Selection of Topics Remains Balanced

One more note before I move on to developing the focus of your content: would you say that the overall curriculum in your educational ministry is well rounded and balanced? Are you attending to the various disciplines within your educational ministry program to make sure students are receiving a healthy diet of biblical studies, theological reflections, spiritual disciplines, ethical considerations, and missional directives? In my former church, I realized that we were not balanced in our approach to educational ministry. After perusing our curriculum materials, I found that a majority of our recent adult studies had encompassed areas involving spiritual formation and discipleship. We had led studies on marriage, parenting, integrity, financial freedom, hope, midlife crises, and living with confidence in the past couple of years. In addition, I felt that our Sunday morning and Wednesday night programs were giving our people the biblical/theological foundations they needed. But where we were lacking was in preparing the saints for ministry and equipping them to share their faith. In the last several years, the church had only led one series on evangelism (a study on Islam). What that congregation really needed was more resources and teaching on leadership and equipping.

This analysis exposed the need for a three-pronged approach to balancing subject matters in educational ministry. This approach involves these areas (described in figure 5):

- biblical/theological foundations (faith, doctrine, and biblical literacy)
- spiritual formation/discipleship (obedience, faithfulness, servanthood, Christian stewardship, prayer, etc.)
- leadership/equipping ministries (learning how to lead in ministry and in vocation, becoming equipped to evangelize, knowing about other religions/worldviews)

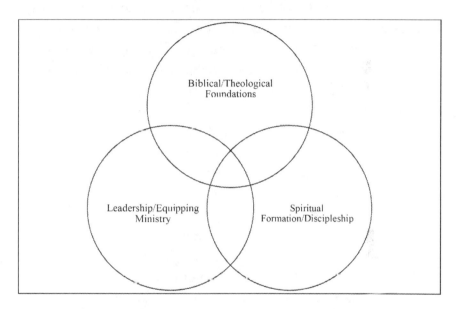

Figure 4: Areas of Emphasis in Educational Ministry

Conclusion

A quote attributed to Henry Kissinger asserts, "If you do not know where you are going, every road will get you nowhere." In instructional design, if we don't know our destination, then we will never get there. This notion is what pressed Kaufman and English (1979) to refer to a needs assessment as a humanizing process that helps us make sure we are using our time and the learners' time in the most effective and efficient ways possible. Oftentimes, we tend to jump the gun in this process and bypass the hard work it takes to ensure that our lessons or messages will be meaningful in the long term, but we should always remember that the quality of our evaluation determines whether or not we hit the target.

Think about it this way. Suppose that you were the captain of a cruise vessel trying to get to the Caribbean islands from Port Canaveral, Florida. If you began your journey two degrees off pace, what would happen? At first, it would not look like you were off course by much, but over time, the distance between your intended target and your actual target would become very noticeable. Likewise, think about your educational targets in your specific educational ministry. Are the people you are ministering to receiving the instruction they need to keep them on course in life and make the right choices according to God's Word? Are you doing what is necessary to arrive at the right destination, or might you be two degrees off? Before you move forward in the instructional design process, make sure that the topics you select are indeed what your target audience needs to hear at that time.

Following through with this process will help you discover *the gaps of most importance* that need to be addressed in your educational ministry. Is this series necessary for your learners? Is it timely for your learners? It's only after you have determined the most important instructional destinations for your context that you can begin to hone in your topic and describe the main theme of your message. From there, you will be able to develop educational goals, essential questions, summative assessments, objectives, lesson strategies/content, and formative evaluation. The following chapters will address these concepts.

Practice Makes Perfect

Duel-Response Survey Worksheet

Directions: Use this worksheet to create some of your own ESOs and develop a corresponding duel-response survey that will evaluate your student's gaps in these areas.

1.) Write down three ESOs that God has put on your heart for learners to take away from your program.

   a. _____

   b. _____

   c. _____

2.) Develop six questions (two for each ESO) for your own duel-responsc survey that will measure the gaps in your educational ministry context.

Instructions. Indicate your level of agreement with the survey questions below (Scale: 1=Strongly disagree; 2=Disagree; 3=Neutral; 4=Agree; 5=Strongly agree).		
Current Performance	Survey Question	Desired Performance
1 2 3 4 5		1 2 3 4 5
1 2 3 4 5		1 2 3 4 5
1 2 3 4 5		1 2 3 4 5
1 2 3 4 5		1 2 3 4 5
1 2 3 4 5		1 2 3 4 5
1 2 3 4 5		1 2 3 4 5
1 2 3 4 5		1 2 3 4 5
1 2 3 4 5		1 2 3 4 5

Practice Makes Perfect

Biblical Literacy Test Worksheet
(Used with permission from Jeff Crawford, 2002)

Directions: Use the following biblical literacy test to measure the biblical deficiencies that may subsist in your students.

Answer all the questions below using the response scale indicated. For questions 1–9, put these biblical events in correct order.

1. Put in *chronological* order the following events (numbering 1–4).
   _____ Isaac's birth
   _____ Judah's exile
   _____ Moses in Egypt
   _____ King Saul's death

2. Put in *chronological* order the following events (numbering 1–4).
   _____ The death of Christ
   _____ Abraham's life
   _____ The coming of the Holy Spirit at Pentecost
   _____ The Old Testament prophets prophesy

3. Place the following people in their correct *chronological* order (numbering 1–5).
   _____ Moses
   _____ Abraham
   _____ David
   _____ Solomon
   _____ Adam

4. Put in *chronological* order the following events from Jesus's life (numbering 1–5).
   _____ The transfiguration
   _____ Turning water into wine
   _____ His baptism

_____ The Sermon on the Mount

_____ Arrest in the garden of Gethsemane

5. Place these events in their correct *biblical* (the order they appear in the Bible) order (numbering 1–5).

_____ The giving of the Law at Mount Sinai

_____ The creation of the heavens and the earth

_____ The fall of man

_____ The Exodus led by Moses

_____ The flood of Noah

6. Put in *chronological* order the following events from Paul's life (numbering 1–4).

_____ Paul's first missionary journey

_____ The stoning of Steven

_____ Paul's Damascus Road experience

_____ Paul's address to the Jerusalem Council

7. Place the following people in their correct *chronological* order (numbering 1–4).

_____ Nebuchadnezzar

_____ Job

_____ Nehemiah

_____ Goliath

8. Place the following events in their correct *biblical* order (numbering 1–5).

_____ The Holy Spirit descends and the people speak in tongues

_____ John has a vision on the island of Patmos

_____ Jesus is baptized in the Jordan River

_____ Paul, Barnabus, and Mark are sent out on a mission by the church

_____ Peter denied that he knows Jesus

9. Place the following events in their correct *biblical* order (numbering 1–4).

_____ Paul's arrest in Jerusalem

_____ Mary's song at Jesus's birth

_____ Nicodemus's conversation about rebirth

_____ Peter's denial of Jesus

For questions 10–28, please put a check (or an *X*) next to the right answer.

10. Which *one* of the following was a disciple of Jesus Christ?

_____ Timothy

_____ Matthew

_____ Paul

_____ Barnabus

_____ Jude

11. Which Bible book contains Paul's missionary journeys?

_____ Ephesians

_____ Galatians

_____ The Corinthians

_____ Acts

12. Which Bible book contains the story of Samson?

_____ Ruth

_____ 1 Samuel

_____ Judges

_____ 1 Kings

13. Which Bible book contains the Sermon on the Mount?

_____ Matthew

_____ Mark

_____ Luke

_____ John

14. Which kingdom fell first?

_____ Israel (northern kingdom)

_____ Judah (southern kingdom)

15. What Bible book comes between Daniel and Joel?

_____ Amos

_____ Isaiah

_____ Hosea

_____ Obadiah

16. Which of the following Bible Books is *not* part of the Pentateuch?

_____ Leviticus

_____ Genesis

_____ Joshua

_____ Numbers

17. Who wrote the majority of the book of Psalms?

_____ Moses

_____ Solomon

_____ David

_____ Paul

18. Of the 66 books of the Bible, how many are in the New Testament?

_____ 27

_____ 37

_____ 39

_____ 29

19. Jesus was crucified during which Jewish festival?

_____ Passover

_____ Hanukkah

_____ Tabernacles

_____ Sabbath

_____ Purim

20. Which of the following statements was said by Jesus *while on the cross?*

_____ "Enter by the narrow gate."

_____ "If this cup cannot pass away from Me unless I drink it, Your will be done."

_____ "Daughters of Jerusalem, do not weep for Me, but weep for yourselves."

_____ "Repent, for the kingdom of heaven is at hand."

21. Which Bible book contains the Passover story?

_____ Acts

_____ Deuteronomy

_____ Exodus

_____ John

22. Which is the first of the Ten Commandments?

_____ You shall not take the name of the Lord your God in vain.

_____ You shall not make for yourself a carved image.

_____ You shall have no other gods before me.

_____ Remember the Sabbath day, to keep it holy.

23. Which of the following was/were *not* present on the night of Jesus's birth?

_____ Angels

_____ Wise men

_____ Shepherds

_____ Joseph

24. Who led the first group of Jews back to Jerusalem from the Babylonian Exile?

_____ Ezra

_____ Nehemiah

_____ Zerubbabel

25. What did God create on the fifth day?
_____ Sea creatures
_____ Land and vegetation
_____ The sun and moon
_____ Land animals

26. Which Bible book would you look in to find wisdom literature?
_____ Revelation
_____ Ecclesiastes
_____ Daniel
_____ Romans

27. Which *one* of the following passages would you refer to when describing man's sinful condition?
_____ Romans 3:23
_____ Romans 6:23
_____ John 3:16
_____ John 1:1

28. Which one of the following passages would you refer to when explaining Jesus's deity?
_____ Romans 3:23
_____ Romans 6:23
_____ John 3:16
_____ John 1:1

For questions 29–35, please write the answer in the blank provided. Please print clearly.

29. During which Jewish festival did the Holy Spirit descend and people speak in tongues? _____.

30. "Though He slay me, yet I will trust in Him" was said by _____.

31. How many plagues did God inflict upon Egypt? _____.

32. What was Abel's occupation? _____.

33. Who wrote the letter to the Philippians? _____.

34. Which gospel is not one of the synoptic gospels? _____.

35. Who led the Hebrew people in the conquest of Canaan? _____.

BIBLICAL LITERACY TEST KEY:

1. *Correct order*: Isaac's birth, Moses in Egypt, King Saul's death, Judah's exile

2. *Correct order*: Abraham's life, the Old Testament prophets prophesy, the death of Christ, the coming of the Holy Spirit at Pentecost

3. *Correct order*: Adam, Abraham, Moses, David, Solomon

4. *Correct order*: His baptism, turning water into wine, the Sermon on the Mount, the Transfiguration, arrest in the Garden of Gethsemane

5. *Correct order*: The creation of the heavens and the earth, the Fall of Man, the flood of Noah, the Exodus led by Moses, the giving of the law at Mount Sinai

6. *Correct order*: The stoning of Steven, Paul's Damascus Road experience, Paul's first missionary journey, Paul's address to the Jerusalem Council

7. *Correct order*: Job, Goliath, Nebuchadnezzar, Nehemiah

8. *Correct order*: Jesus is baptized in the Jordan River, Peter denied that he knows Jesus, the Holy Spirit descends and the people speak in tongues, Paul, Barnabus, and Mark are sent out on a mission by the church, John has a vision on the Island of Patmos

9. *Correct order*: Mary's song at Jesus birth, Nicodemus' conversation about rebirth, Peter's denial of Jesus, Paul's arrest in Jerusalem

10. Matthew
11. Acts
12. Judges
13. Matthew
14. Israel
15. Hosea
16. Joshua
17. David
18. 27

19. Passover
20. "Daughters of Jerusalem, do not weep for Me, but weep for yourselves ..."
21. Exodus
22. You shall have no other gods before me
23. Wise men
24. Zerubbabel
25. Sea creatures
26. Ecclesiastes
27. Romans 3:23
28. John 1:1
29. Pentecost
30. Job
31. 10
32. Shepherd
33. Paul
34. John
35. Joshua

Sources

Burton, J. K., and P. F. Merrill. "Needs Assessment: Goals, Needs, and Priorities." In *Instructional Design: Principles and Applications*, edited by L. J. Briggs, K. L. Gustafson, and M. H. Tillman, 17-44. England Cliffs, New Jersey: Educational Technology, 1991.

Crawford, J. S. (2002). *An Analysis of the Biblical Literacy of High School Students in Conservative Evangelical Schools.*" EdD diss., Southern Baptist Theological Seminary, 2002. Retrieved from ProQuest Dissertations and Theses.

English, F. *Deciding What to Teach and Test: Developing, Aligning, and Leading the Curriculum.* 3rd ed. Thousand Oaks, California: Corwin, 2010.

Gunter, M. A., T. H. Estes, and S. L. Mintz. *Instruction: A Models Approach.* 5th ed. Boston, Massachusetts: Pearson, 2007.

Kaufman, R. A., and F. W. English. *Needs Assessment: Concept and Application.* Englewood Cliffs, New Jersey: Educational Technology, 1979.

Pazmino, R. W. *Foundational Issues in Christian Education.* 3rd ed. Grand Rapids, Michigan: Baker Academic, 2008.

Richards, L. O., and G. O. Bredfeldt. *Creative Bible Teaching.* Chicago, Illinois: Moody Bible Institute, 1998.

Slavin, R. E. *Educational Psychology: Theory and Practice.* 9th ed. Boston, Massachusetts: Pearson, 2009.

Smith, P. L., and T. J. Ragan. *Instructional Design.* 3rd ed. Upper Saddle River, New Jersey: Wiley & Sons, Inc, 2005.

Vygotsky, L. S. *Mind in Society: The Development of Higher Psychological Processes*. Compiled by M. Cole, V. John-Steiner, S. Scribner, & E. Souberman. Cambridge, Massachusetts: Harvard University Press, 1978.

Watkins, R., M. W. Meiers, and Y. L. Visser. *A Guide to Assessing Needs: Essential Tools for Collecting Information, Making Decisions, and Achieving Development Results*. Washington, D.C.: International Bank for Reconstruction and Development, 2012.

Wiggins, G., and J. McTighe. *Understanding by Design*. 2nd ed. Alexandria, Virginia: ASCD, 2005.

4

DEFINE THE FOCUS OF THE CONTENT

To define the essential content for the lesson, you need to have a deep understanding of the intended learning. If you find yourself able to only list the facts and concepts that students should know, without placing them into any larger learning picture, you should work on your own understanding before you try to plan instruction.

—Connie Moss and Susan Brookhart

In your teaching show integrity, seriousness and soundness of speech that cannot be condemned, so that those who oppose you may be ashamed because they have nothing bad to say about us.

—Titus 2:7b–8 (NIV)

British athlete Jonathan Edwards considered himself to be merely a "skinny-looking, very ordinary guy." However, on August 7, 1995, he proved himself to be anything but ordinary. It was on this day, during the track and field World Championships, that he broke the world record for the longest triple jump in history (an incredible 18.29 meters or just over 60 feet). His mark in the sand still stands today over twenty years later. For those unfamiliar with the triple jump, it is an event in which athletes run down a track that leads to a sandpit. There are three phases required for this event (hence the name). First, after gathering speed, an athlete will jump off one foot then land on the same foot and jump again. The third jump requires the athlete to jump off the opposite foot and travel as far into the sandpit as humanly possible.

Despite breaking the world record for his event, Edwards's eyes were fixed on yet another feat, winning a gold medal in the Olympics. In 1996, Edwards entered the Barcelona Olympics as the clear favorite to win that illustrious accolade. However, it was not to be. His best mark fell just short of American athlete Kenny Harris. It was the longest jump ever to not win gold. This meant that Edwards would have to settle for the silver medal and wait four years for another shot at the Sydney Olympics in 2000. His tenacity paid off; as he would go on to win the gold medal that year while still striving to break his own record. After retiring several years later, Edwards spoke about what he hoped his achievements would do for future generations. He insisted that his accomplishments have the potential to inspire young athletes as they look at his mark in the sand and think, "If he can do it, I can do it too" (Rowbottom, 2015).

In your educational ministry, do students have a *mark in the sand* that they are striving to reach both intellectually and spiritually? Are they being inspired to grow and accomplish specific goals that you have put in place for them? Do they have visible examples of what "good work looks like," or are they left in the dark, guessing what you expect from them? If you want to be an effective teacher, then you must learn to define the expectations you have for your students and clearly communicate those expectations on a regular basis. When students see the line or the mark you want them to reach, they will inevitably work harder to get there. If there is no mark, their motivation to learn will dwindle. Put simply, it's our job to help them see where they are aiming and point them in the right direction.

The prior chapters of this book were meant to help you analyze your learners and the learning environment, as well as perform a needs analysis to determine the gaps of most importance that must be bridged in your educational ministry. Your next goal will be to bring focus to your instructional design by encapsulating the essence of your topic and creating educational goals that will describe what you want students to know, understand, or be able to do as a result of your instruction.

Gauging the needs of others and determining educational goals based on those evaluations are two ideals that I believe the early apostles understood and applied on a regular basis. Consider how the apostle Paul in his first letter to Timothy incorporated goals into an analysis of the people of Ephesus and their needs. Listen to his words in 1 Timothy 1:3–7 (NIV).

> As I urged you when I went into Macedonia, stay there in Ephesus so that you may command certain people not to teach false doctrines any longer or to devote themselves to myths and endless genealogies. Such things promote controversial speculations rather than advancing God's work—which is by faith. The goal of this command is love, which comes from a pure heart and a good conscience and a sincere faith. Some have departed from these and have turned to meaningless talk. They want to be teachers of the law, but they do not know what they are talking about or what they so confidently affirm.

As you read through this passage, what do you notice about Paul's assessment of the spiritual needs or gaps of certain Ephesian individuals? First of all, you should observe that he is exposing those within the Christian community who were teaching false doctrines and devoting themselves to myths and endless genealogies. Their obvious *gap* in spiritual maturity was resulting in controversial speculations and meaningless discourses. They wanted so badly to be good teachers, but they didn't have a correct understanding of what they were talking about. Notice that Paul used the word *goal* to indicate what he really desired for these people. His goal was not to embarrass them or condemn them but to correct them by showing love. Love comes from a pure heart, a good conscience, and sincere faith. This Scripture shows us how Paul not only identified a clear *gap*, he also suggested a clear *goal*.

So what does this mean for us in our educational ministry contexts today? How can we fill the gaps that are observed in our students? This chapter will help you begin to answer these questions by encouraging you to develop an overarching statement that embodies the main theme that every lesson will unpack in some fashion. Once this is accomplished, you will need to construct educational goals that will be tied to a specific learning domain. This will determine the type of understanding that will be required from your students. Lastly, you will develop a summative assessment that will be used to verify whether or not they actually learned what you desired.

Focusing on the Main Theme and Essential Questions

If you were to review an old syllabus from college, what are the first few items that you would see at the top of the front page? In most syllabi, it will be the name of the course, the professor's name, and the course description. The course description is very important as it is the main theme (the biggest idea of the big ideas) or, as Wiggins and McTighte (2005) designate, a "linchpin of education." A linchpin is a devise that holds a wheel in place on an axle. Similarly, the main theme of a unit or course is essential for understanding the content as it holds everything together.

Wiggins and McTighte warn that if your group does not grasp what your main theme is or is unable to use it to hold together related content, they will be left with only bits and pieces of information that will not take them anywhere. So all the lessons within your unit or series should be related to the main theme and progress it in some way. The authors go on to explain that this will help learners answer these questions: What is most important here? How do the pieces connect? What should I pay most attention to? Answering these questions will allow them connect the dots and provide a conceptual "lens" that brings depth to the content being examined. To this end, Moss and Brookhart (2012) propose that teachers should consider where each lesson resides in a larger learning trajectory and identify the next steps students must take to move toward overarching understandings and educational goals. This is why your main theme or course description is so important.

The description of your main theme should be four to five sentences long (about a paragraph). It should be clear and concise so everyone can understand the purpose and the focus of the class. Somewhere in your statement, tell your students why they are taking this course and how the content will benefit them in the future. In other words, "What's in it for them?" You will also want to eliminate any vague or unclear words (e.g., this class will empower you, it will give you a hands-on experience, we will raise issues, it will be intensive, this is a unique experience). The description you create will set the tone for the development of educational goals.

Once you have a firm grasp on your main theme, proceed by consulting a wide range of material involving what experts or commentators have to say about your topic. This will allow you to familiarize yourself with common terminology so you can begin to understand what should be involved for the task ahead (Smith and Ragan, 2005). Your search should lead to the development of a list of questions about your topic that you want answered or you want your students to be able to answer. For example, which biblical authors address this subject, and what do they say? What are the most difficult terms or concepts that need to be explained in more detail? How do these ideas fit together? Wiggins and McTighte (2005) refer to questions like these as **essential questions**. Essential questions can be described as doorways through which we can explore the key concepts, themes, theories, issues, and problems that reside within the content. They push us to the heart or the essence of the subject matter. They cause genuine and relevant inquiry and provoke deep thought. They provide a lens through which all knowledge and activities will be processed.

Think about it this way. If you were only able to ask your students several questions about your course or unit of instruction after it ended, what would those questions be? These questions should deliver the main point of what you want them to learn right now. An example of an essential question for a biblical studies class may be: why are the "heroes of the faith" mentioned in Hebrews 11 important for Christians today to emulate? That is a big, overarching question that would guide your instruction. From this, you would be able to break each biblical character down from that chapter and discuss how he or she displayed faith in life. Then you could connect this to your students' lives by discussing what the next chapter says in Hebrews 12:1 (NIV): "Therefore, since we are surrounded by such a great cloud of witnesses, let us throw off everything that hinders and the sin that so easily entangles. And let us run with perseverance the race marked out for us."

So what will the essential questions for your course or unit of study be? After consulting your resources, come up with several questions that undergird your main theme. Your questions may be realized through a consideration of these three arenas (as adapted from Wiggins and McTighte).

- *Questions involving your topic that recur throughout all our lives.* These questions are broad in scope and timeless by nature (e.g., what is justice?). People may change their minds in response to reflection and experience concerning such questions as they go through life. There is no right or wrong answer to these questions.
- *Questions involving your topic that deal with important ideas and inquiries within a discipline.* Think about questions that are historically important and have been discussed for generations. What are areas within your topic that are debated by experts? What are they currently trying to find out about your topic? What will help your students make sense of important but complicated ideas and knowledge? Those areas may be worth examining.
- *Questions that will most engage a specific and diverse set of learners.* What will hook and hold the attention of your specific students? As Wiggins and McTighte suggest, some

adult questions may be important in the grand scheme of things, but they hold no apparent relevance or interest to teenage students. In other words, consider your audience.

Whatever your unit is about, make sure to design it around answering your essential questions or explaining the main concepts (e.g., the sinful nature, sanctification, the tabernacle). It is with these questions and themes that you will be able to begin to develop educational goals.

Focusing on Educational Goals

In his book, *Educational Psychology: Theory and Practice,* Robert Slavin (2009) states that students often live up or down to the expectations that their teachers have for them. This should signify to teachers that they must be intentional about creating attainable educational goals that can be used to measure student success. The more focused these goals are and the more teachers specify what they want students to accomplish, the easier it will be to select and arrange learning experiences for students and evaluate their performance in accordance with those goals (Gunter, Estes, and Mintz, 2007).

Smith and Ragan (2005) define **educational goals** (also referred to as learning goals or terminal objectives) as statements of purpose or intention. They include the knowledge or skills that your learners should possess at the conclusion of an instructional unit or course. People often confuse educational goals with instructional objectives because their wording is similar (both describe what students should be able to do after instruction is given), but they are actually very different in nature. I will discuss instructional objectives in a later chapter, but for now, what you need to know is that objectives as subparts of educational goals. Smith and Ragan add that educational goals are more general and less precise than instructional objectives. A teacher may end up having four or five total educational goals for a unit of instruction, but each lesson may have several objectives.

It's also worth noting that educational goals are intended outcomes for students, not process statements that describe how they will get to a certain outcome. Gunter, Estes, and Mintz (2007) illustrate this notion by relating it to the building of a new house. If you were to build a new house, there would be a specific process for building that house. The foundation must be laid before the walls can go up. Then scaffolding can be used to install the roof. Texture and paint will be added to the walls along with electrical and pluming needs. These are all process statements. On the other hand, here are some statements that describe characteristics or outcomes of the completed house: the house will contain two fireplaces, the front of the house will face south, and all the windows will be constructed of double-plane glass. Do you see the difference? It is the same with educational goals; they are the intended outcomes of instruction.

Crafting Educational Goals

Many organizations today embrace the creation of SMART goals (goals that are specific, measurable, attainable, relevant/realistic, and timely). In his book, *Designing and Teaching Learning Goals and Objectives*, Robert Marzano (2009) expands this list by suggesting that teachers create clear and specific educational goals at just the right level of difficulty. He believes students are most motivated by educational goals that they perceive as difficult but not too difficult. In other words, they want to be challenged, but they do not want to be discouraged either. Their perception about levels of difficulty will be affected by their current state of knowledge, their beliefs about what causes achievement, and their opinions of their own abilities.

Let me illustrate this by describing an experience I had as a middle school math teacher. One day, I was teaching my seventh grade math class about the lateral surface area of prisms. I taught the concept from our textbook curriculum, explained the steps that needed to be completed, and even had the students practice problems on the board. Despite this, there was one student in my class who didn't even want to try. She was convinced that the material was too difficult to master. For most of the class period, she stared at the wall in disbelief. Her negative opinion of her abilities and her frustration over past geometry failures had convinced her that she would not be able to figure out how to do it. After observing her frustrations for several minutes, I decided to go through each step directly with her one more time. This time, she got it! She realized that it was a difficult concept, but if she really applied herself, she could get it. When producing educational goals, teachers must decipher this tension and help students reach their potential.

Keeping these things in mind, teachers should craft their educational goals in terms of what they hope their students will *know, understand,* or be able to *do* after the unit of instruction has run its course. Gunter, Estes, and Mintz (2007) call this the KUD (know, understand, be able to do) method. On a quick note, the use of the word *understand* in educational goals has come under scrutiny in recent years as some view it as too vague. Students cannot easily demonstrate understanding (Marzano, 2009). I would agree if these were being written as instructional objectives, but for general educational goals, I see the usage as acceptable.

The first format you can use to describe educational goals, according to Gunter, Estes, and Mintz (2007), involves what "students will know." These goals will detail the facts, concepts, and procedures that students must master to successfully complete the series or unit (the stuff they need to know). Choosing this format will force you to focus on particular types of knowledge that will be given during instruction. In other words, this type of goal will remind you of the essential information that is worth being taught. This will help prevent unnecessary tangents. An example might be: students will know the reasons why the Bible is relevant in today's culture.

Secondly, you may want to focus your educational goals on the phrase "students will understand." Knowing the stuff may not always be enough; they must make sense of the information. Students oftentimes need to interweave their newly gained knowledge into abstract, transferable ideas. Much of the reason for this is the fact that there is often too much information to absorb in any given lesson or unit of instruction. This educational goal format helps teachers organize facts, concepts, and skills into manageable chunks so students can see the big picture. The more they understand, the more they will apply to their lives. Wiggins and McTighte (2005) add that understanding is about transfer. It requires the ability to transfer what we have learned to new and sometimes confusing settings. While knowledge is about facts, understanding provides coherence and meaning to those facts. We can judge when to and when not to use what we know. An example of this format would be: students will understand how the Holy Spirit enables men and women to interpret Scripture.

The third form of educational goals begins with "students will be able to." These educational goals are more practical and focus on student behaviors, and they incorporate the tasks that will be required to reveal how well knowledge has been transferred. They also detail what observable and measurable behaviors students will demonstrate at the end of a unit of instruction. An example of this format would be: students will be able to demonstrate that they can effectively interpret and apply a passage of Scripture.

Classifying Educational Goals

Once you have composed your educational goals for a course or unit, it is valuable to identify the type of **learning outcome** the goal represents. The learning outcome involves the kind of learning that will be required from your students. Some learning tasks are substantially different from others in terms of amount and kind of cognitive effort required in learning (Smith and Ragan, 2005). For instance, asking your students to memorize John 1:1–14 is a different task than having them learn how to defend the doctrine of the Trinity. Memorization involves attention and perseverance, as a particular type of mental effort and rehearsal. In memorizing Scripture, an individual must break the task up into smaller pieces, memorize one piece at a time, and then put all the pieces together as it is recited. However, learning to defend the doctrine of the Trinity will require a different kind of mental effort. Unlike the memorizing tasks (which are always the same), the appropriate principles and sequences for doctrinal defense will vary. Teachers may guide students in their learning by reminding them of appropriate principles, giving them practice exercises, and offering feedback as to whether the defenses they can give at the end of your instruction are accurate.

Given the complex nature of knowledge and understanding, I have found it beneficial to classify educational goals at what I call their macro and micro levels. The macro level involves the part of the human psyche that you are trying to reach through your educational goal. Do you want your students to leave with certain cognitive imprints on their minds (i.c., facts and details)? Would you rather have them process your lesson(s) internally and make them want to change something about their lives? Or maybe you want to teach them how to do something practically (i.e., actions and skills)? These questions (involving the macro level of educational goals) are general in nature and look at the big picture of what you want to accomplish. On the other hand, the micro level of educational goals looks specifically at the type of knowledge you want to impart and the cognitive processes that students must transcend in order to achieve your educational goals.

The Macro Level of Educational Goals

In 1949, Benjamin Bloom enlisted several educational specialists from across the United States to aid in developing congruency among faculty at various universities when it came to educational goals/objectives and the development of tests. Their efforts resulted in the development of a taxonomy or framework for classifying statements of what students are expected to learn as a result of instruction (Krathwohl, 2002). This formation is now widely known as **Bloom's Taxonomy**. Bloom's work, along with his colleagues, delineated three major domains of learning: the cognitive domain, the affective domain, and the psychomotor domain (also known as the behavioral domain). These three domains serve as the macro level or general level of educational goals. As stated above, figuring out which domain you are aiming for will help you determine which part of the human psyche you are trying to influence.

Richards and Bredfeldt (1998) condense Bloom's three domains by stating that they reach one's head (cognitive thinking), heart (attitudes and emotions), and hands (behaviors, actions, and skills). To this end, cognitive domains involve one's thinking abilities (knowing essential facts, terminology, and details). For biblical studies courses, teachers hope to impart biblical knowledge to students so they will be able to grasp its significance. The affective domain looks to influence a student's values and attitudes, or as Richards and Bredfeldt designate its purpose: "to inspire, touch the emotions, change or challenge an attitude, affect a personal value choice, or engender commitment to an ideal or belief" (p. 138). In other words, think about how your educational goals can bring people to the point where they develop new convictions and beliefs based on your instruction. Lastly, the behavioral domain hopes to stimulate a response to the content being presented. What skills will they need to excel, and how will they demonstrate their proficiency? How will their lives be different because of your instruction?

The Micro Level of Educational Goals

Krathwohl (2002) explains that cognitive educational goals describing intended learning outcomes as a result of instruction are usually framed in terms of: 1.) subject matter content; 2.) a description of what is to be done with or to that content. Consequently, educational goal statements will usually contain a noun or noun phrase (the subject matter) and a verb or verb phrase (the cognitive processes). An example of this is in the following educational goal. "The students will be able to explain the three main themes of the book of John: signs, belief, and life (as discerned from John 20:30–31)." In this case, the noun or subject matter is "the three main themes of the book of John," and the verb or cognitive process involved is "explain."

As educators, we should hope that our subject matter content (or the noun of the educational goal) is not only retained by our students but also transferred or applied by them as well. According to Mayer (2002), retention involves "the ability to remember material at some later time in much the same way it was presented during instruction" (p. 226). We want students to remember what they have learned. However, transfer involves using that knowledge to solve new problems, answer new questions, or facilitate learning new subject matter. Part of the genius of Bloom's Taxonomy is that it helps teachers broaden a typical educational goal to embrace the promotion of knowledge transfer. To this end, Bloom and his team developed three categories (later a fourth was added) that describe the types of knowledge that we hope to pass on to our students. This is commonly known as the knowledge dimension. A description of these is listed below adapted from Krathwohl (2002).

- *Factual knowledge*: the basic elements that students must know to be acquainted with a discipline or solve problems in it (e.g., terms, details, elements).
- *Conceptual knowledge*: the interrelationships among the basic elements within a larger structure that enable them to function together (e.g., classification, categories, theories, models, structures).
- *Procedural knowledge*: how to do something; methods of inquiry; and criteria for using skills, algorithms, techniques, and methods (e.g., subject specific skills, techniques, methods, procedures).
- *Metacognitive knowledge*: knowledge of cognition in general as well as awareness and knowledge of one's own cognition; strategies for learning how to learn (e.g., organizational strategies, rehearsal strategies, performance strategies).

In order to promote higher forms of thinking in education, Bloom's original taxonomy (before it was revised forty-five years after its conception) also provided definitions of six major cognitive processes (the verbs of educational goals): knowledge, comprehension, application, analysis, synthesis, and evaluation. These categories are ordered from simple to complex. The premise is that it will take a deeper level of learning to *evaluate* something than it will to simply *remember* it. The revised list makes minor changes to the original. This includes renaming several of them and reordering two of them. Bloom's Taxonomy now states that students should remember, understand, apply, analyze, evaluate, and create. A summary of definitions for each of these and corresponding verbs for educational goals can be found below (adapted from Krathwohl, 2002).

1.) *Remember.* Retrieving knowledge from long-term memory (other possible verbs: recognizing, identifying, recalling, retrieving).

2.) *Understand.* Determining the meaning of instructional messages, including oral, written, and graphic communication (other possible verbs: interpreting, exemplifying, classifying, clarifying, summarizing, inferring, comparing, contrasting, explaining).

3.) *Apply.* Carrying out or using a procedure in a given situation (other possible verbs: executing, implementing, using, utilizing, carrying out).

4.) *Analyze.* Breaking material into its constituent parts and determine how the parts relate to one another and to an overall structure or purpose (other possible verbs: differentiating, organizing, attributing, discriminating, distinguishing, focusing, selecting, integrating, structuring, deconstructing).

5.) *Evaluate.* Making judgments based on criteria and standards (other possible verbs: coordinating, detecting, monitoring, testing, judging).

6.) *Create.* Putting elements together to form a coherent or functional whole; reorganize elements into a new pattern or structure (other possible verbs: generating, planning, producing, hypothesizing, designing, constructing).

Smith and Ragan (2005) add that categorizing different types of learning is useful for teachers as they create their lesson plans. This encourages them to aim their goals toward "higher order, more mentally demanding outcomes" (p. 79). So don't settle for simple or lower levels of learning; aim for deeper learning transfer. Ask these questions from Moss and Brookhart (2012) when developing educational goals: What thought-demanding processes will allow my students to build on what they already know and can do? What kinds of thinking will promote deep understanding and skill development so that students can analyze, reshape, explain, extrapolate from, apply, and build on what they already know? In table 3, you will see how you can put together the noun and the verb according to Bloom's Revised Taxonomy and begin to see a change in your educational ministry context.

The Knowledge Dimension	The Cognitive Processes Dimension					
	Remember	Understand	Apply	Analyze	Evaluate	Create
Factual Knowledge	Beginner					
Conceptual Knowledge						
Procedural Knowledge				Expert		
Metacognitive Knowledge						
	Simple				Complex	

Table 3: Bloom's Taxonomy's Cognitive Processes and Knowledge Dimensions

Assessing Educational Goals

Before you ever start teaching a lesson, it is important to determine how you will evaluate student achievement. Unfortunately, this is a step many biblically based educational programs often put on the backburner or completely omit. In his book, *Why Nobody Learns Much of Anything at Church: And How to Fix It*, Thom Schultz

(1993) explains that this may be due to the fact that many biblical instructors are afraid of what they will see or hear. They are under the impression that evaluation and assessments will only give people a chance to complain. However, if we truly care about helping our people become more like Christ, then we must find ways to verify that it is happening. As I was taught in college, "when teachers assume, they structure everything on sand."

In educational settings, there are two main types of assessment: summative and formative. These will be covered in more detail in a later chapter, but for the purposes of this section, it is pertinent to understand that formative assessments are executed during or after each lesson, while summative assessments take place at the end of an instructional unit. Final summative assessments will have much to say about what you design. Where do you want your students to be when they complete your class? If you don't know where you are going, then how will you get there? In short, summative assessments help you think with the end in mind and allow your end game to dictate what you spend your energy on. As Dick, Carey, and Carey (2009) indicate, assessments inform us just how well learners were able to achieve each educational goal and also which components of the instruction worked well and which ones need to be revised. So at the end of your unit or course, will you give your students a test, have them turn in reflection journals, write essays, or complete projects and portfolios? Think about your end game, and decide now how you will evaluate the educational goals before considering the scope and sequence of the content that you will incorporate in your instructional design.

Conclusion

A needs assessment may bring to light areas that need to be addressed, but those areas will be lost in translation without the development of a main theme and educational goals that will generate clarity for both teachers and students. Think of this process like a funnel that is wide at the top and narrow at the bottom. Instructional design may be wide and general at first, but every step becomes more specific. At the top of your funnel will be the big needs (gaps) of your students. Moving deeper, you will begin to focus on your main theme/course description and then on to the development of essential questions and attainable educational goals. The number of educational goals you end up with will be dependent upon the size of the gap you are trying to close. You may end up with five or six or just two. Sometimes, you will be able to communicate an educational goal in one lesson, but other times, it will take two or three lessons dedicated to a single concept. Clear targets are important for every educational ministry as they help improve the chances of retention and transfer. As Gunter, Estes, and Mintz (2007) state, "Without clearly articulated targets, teachers and students will have difficulty traversing the road to student learning" (p. 42). However, you can't stop with simply making a goal. You need to examine the type of learning that will be required from your students so you will be able to create a summative assessment that will measure whether the students actually learned something or let it go in one ear and out the other.

In the next chapter, I will explain how having a firm grasp on your educational goals will help you make informed decisions about the content you choose to deliver to your students and how to sequence that content in a logical way that will allow for connections to be made between concepts. The key is to move your students along in the process and move toward achieving the educational goals. In other words, keep your eyes on the prize!

Practice Makes Perfect

Bringing Focus to your Content Worksheet

Directions: Below you will find some educational goal statements. Decide which learning domain they belong to (cognitive, affective, or behavioral) by placing a check in the appropriate blank to the side.

Cognitive Affective Behavioral

1.) Students will be able to distinguish the similarities and differences between the four Gospels.   _____ _____ _____

2.) Students will be able to effectively utilize the tools of effective biblical interpretation.   _____ _____ _____

3.) Students will understand the crucial role of the Old Testament Prophets during the time of the Exile.   _____ _____ _____

4.) Students will hold a deep respect for Scripture as God's Word and the standard for faith and practice.   _____ _____ _____

5.) Students will appreciate the complex process involved in the creation of the biblical canon.   _____ _____ _____

6.) Students will be able to explain the relevance of Jesus's teachings for today's Christians.   _____   _____   _____

7.) Students will understand and appropriate the attitudes and teachings of Paul and the other early apostles.   _____   _____   _____

8.) Students will incorporate the spiritual disciplines (e.g., fasting, silence and solitude, biblical meditation) into their daily lives.   _____   _____   _____

9.) Students will produce an evangelical response to cultural issues faced in America today.   _____   _____   _____

10.) Students will develop a constructive methodology for teaching through the Old Testament Prophets.   _____   _____   _____

Sources

Dick, W. O., L. Carey, and J. O. Carey. *The Systematic Design of Instruction*. 7th ed. Englewood Cliffs, New Jersey: Merrill, 2011.

Duvall, J. S., and J. D. Hays. *Grasping God's Word: A Hands on Approach to Reading, Interpreting, and Applying the Bible*. Grand Rapids, Michigan: Zondervan, 2001.

Earl, L. M. *Assessment as Learning: Using Classroom Assessment to Maximize Student Learning*. Thousand Oaks, California: Corwin Press, Inc., 2003.

Gunter, M. A., T. H. Estes, and S. L. Mintz. *Instruction: A Models Approach*. 5th ed. Boston, Massachusetts: Pearson, 2007.

Krathwohl, D. "A Revision of Bloom's Taxonomy: An Overview." *Theory into Practice*, 41 (Autumn 2002): 212-218. Retrieved from EBSCO*host*.

Mayer, R. E. "Rote Verses Meaningful Learning." *Theory into Practice*, 41 (Autumn 2002): 226-232. Retrieved from EBSCO*host*.

Marzano, R. J. *Designing and Teaching Learning Goals and Objectives*. Bloomington, Indiana: Marzano Research, 2009.

Moss, C. M., and S. M. Brookhart. *Learning Targets: Helping Students Aim for Understanding in Today's Lesson*. Alexandria, Virginia: ASCD, 2012.

Richards, L. O., and G. O. Bredfeldt. *Creative Bible Teaching*. Chicago, Illinois: Moody Bible Institute, 1998.

Robinson, H. *Biblical Preaching: The Development and Delivery of Expository Messages.* 2nd ed. Grand Rapids, Michigan: Baker Academic, 2001.

Rowbottom, M. "Twenty years on the extraordinary triple jump world record of a 'skinny-looking, very ordinary guy.'" *Inside the Games*, August 3, 2015. http://www.insidethegames.biz/articles/1029094/twenty-years-on-the-extraordinary-triple-jump-world-record-of-a-skinny-looking-very-ordinary-guy

Slavin, R. E. *Educational Psychology: Theory and Practice.* 9th ed. Boston, Massachusetts: Pearson, 2009.

Smith, P. L., and T. J. Ragan. *Instructional Design.* 3rd ed. Upper Saddle River, New Jersey: Wiley & Sons, Inc., 2005.

Wiggins, G., and J. McTighte. *Understanding by Design.* 2nd ed. Alexandria, Virginia: ASCD, 2005.

Willhite, K., and S. M. Gibson. *The Big Idea of Biblical Preaching: Connecting the Bible to People.* Grand Rapids, Michigan: Baker Academic, 2003.

5

ESTABLISH THE SCOPE AND SEQUENCE

Learners on all levels are bombarded with more and more knowledge, which they must synthesize. No one, practicing professional or any level student, can learn all there is to learn, nor should they expected to do so. Increasingly difficult decisions must be made concerning what is to be taught, to whom, and to what degree, how, and (perhaps most importantly), why?

—Bruce Ledford and Philip Sleeman

Ezra had devoted himself to the study and observance of the Law of the Lord, and to teaching its decrees and laws in Israel.

—Ezra 7:10 (NIV)

For my first semester as a Christian high school educator, I was asked to teach a course overviewing the gospels. I was excited about this new endeavor, but I quickly discovered that it would be more difficult than I anticipated, as the course did not include any textbooks, notes, or any other supplemental materials that I could utilize. Instead, I was expected to acquire or create these materials on my own. I felt a little overwhelmed at first and unsure of the direction I should go with the class. So I pulled together the notes that I had amassed over the years, and I examined the commentaries and books I owned involving the subject matter. From there, I sought to organize the first month of lessons that would include the history and background surrounding the gospels. After the first two weeks of school, I asked the students how they were feeling about the class, and they were honest enough to tell me that I was overwhelming them with too much information and they were having trouble keeping up with me. They went on to ask if I could trim the content down and present it at their level (they felt I was teaching a college course when they were only juniors in high school). So I swallowed my pride and pivoted on how I presented the material. I made some tough decisions about the breadth and depth of the content (often referred to as the scope and sequence). The process provided me with a crash course on how to concentrate on the essential content or what is really important. I figured out how to search for the big ideas that would guide the class for the remainder of the semester.

In your educational ministry, once you have defined your main theme and educational goals, turn your attention to the **scope and sequence of instruction** so you will avoid the mistakes I made when I first started out in education. The scope of instruction involves what exactly will be taught during a given period of time. The goal in determining the scope is to ensure that what is being taught is truly chipping away at the "gaps" in your students. The challenge in this is avoiding information, ideas, or concepts that are irrelevant to the educational goals (Smith and Ragan, 2005). As Schultz (1993) suggests, a big teaching blunder we often make is thinking that more is better. We try to cram so much information into our people's minds that they become unable to figure out what is essential and what is not essential. The sequence of instruction, on the other hand, has to do with the order in which the content will be presented. Wiggins and McTighte (2005) reveal that understandings are organized in chunks or segments. This means we must determine what content needs to be included in each segment of instruction for learners to achieve the educational goals.

Even though the Bible was not written as a textbook on education, I believe we can glean principles of masterful teaching from its contents. Another example of this comes from King Solomon who was considered one of the wisest men to ever walk the face of this earth. In Ecclesiastes 12:9–10 (NIV), he states, "Not only was the Teacher wise, but he also imparted knowledge to the people. He pondered and searched out and set in order many proverbs. The Teacher searched to find just the right words, and what he wrote was upright and true." Isn't it interesting that Solomon wrote that *the Teacher* searched out for the right proverbs to teach and spent time putting concepts in an order that would make sense? His goal in doing so was to impart the right knowledge that the people needed, so he searched to find the right words that would impact them the most. That is what scope and sequence is all about.

In this chapter, you will discover how to determine the scope and sequence for your unit or course of study. What content needs to be included, and what should be excluded? In what order should the concepts be presented? Gaining an understanding of this will help you break down subject matter into smaller parts so you can identify what students will need in order to accomplish your educational goals and complete the summative assessments. This is the last step in instructional or front-end analysis (the macro level of unit development) before you can move on to specific lesson planning.

The Scope of Instruction

Establishing the scope of instruction involves making discriminations about the content that will be presented under the umbrella of your main theme, essential questions, and educational goals. To help differentiate between essential and nonessential content, I suggest emulating Wiggins and McTighte's (2005) framework for clarifying content. In their minds, content choices should rest on three tiers of importance.

The first tier is "knowledge that students should be only familiar with." Because there is often too much information available for any given subject and we can't teach it all, we must identify knowledge that students should be exposed to but not necessarily be expected to fully understand. This may include certain reading assignments, lecture topics, or encounters that are broad in nature (broad-brush knowledge). If through your research, you discover something that is important but not necessary, consider at least mentioning it, but do not expect them to know it in depth.

Let me give you an example. Several years ago, I taught a two-day seminar on the "doctrine of humanity" to a group of Christian school teachers. One of my goals was to help them differentiate between biblical and unbiblical views of humanity. To do so, I broke the class up into several groups and had each group read an article about humanism, transhumanism, or Freudian psychology. After reading through their given view and discussing it in light of the Bible, each group was to explain to the rest of the class what was learned. Did each group gain a full understanding of each view? Probably not, but they were at least exposed to what each view believes even though they would not understand it in depth. There were other views that we didn't even have time to discuss, so I had to differentiate between what I thought was essential and what was nonessential.

The second tier of possible content involves knowledge, skills, or concepts that have connective and transfer power, within this unit and with other units of study on related topics. In other words, what are possible areas in your content that will be applicable to past classes or future classes? Whatever you determine those things are, they will be worth an investment of time. For instance, if you want to teach a class about the New Testament, it would be advisable to spend time discussing the Old Testament sacrificial system. One cannot understand Jesus's sacrifice as the Passover Lamb without knowing the importance of animal sacrifices in the Old Testament. These connective concepts can be taught in both Old and New Testament courses.

A third tier of content knowledge that you will encounter involves the selection of the big ideas that are at the heart of the subject and anchor the unit or course. **Big ideas** are the things that bind each lesson together and help students make connections between each concept. They are the main concepts that biblical authors focus on and that you should pass on to your students. I was first exposed to the concept of big ideas when I was taking my first master's degree class about educational theory. In that class, my professor used to always ask, "What do you want your students to carry with them for the rest of their lives?" I have never forgotten this, and I am constantly grappling with its implications because the reality is that students will only remember fifteen to twenty percent of what teachers say during any particular lesson. Master teachers will take into consideration which fifteen to twenty percent they want students to know, and they will constantly drive home those points. These concepts are your big ideas.

So where do our big ideas come from? Discovering the answer to this question is paramount for Christian educators whose main source is the Word of God. If we believe that the Bible is the inspired, infallible, and authoritative Word of God and that it contains living commands and teachings from God, then we will surely want to represent it accurately (Willhite and Gibson, 1998). We will have to be true to what the Word says and glean our big ideas from it. Unfortunately, this does not always happen. I have seen too many biblical instructors in recent times stretch the truth of God's Word to fit their own agenda.

This is why we should always keep in the back of our minds what Moses wrote in Deuteronomy 32:47a (NIV), as it pertains to God's commands: "They are not just idle words for you—they are your life." The apostle Paul's encouragement in 2 Timothy 3:16–17 also reminds us that all Scripture came from God and it is useful for teaching, rebuking, correcting, and training in righteousness. These verses serve as a reminder to us as Christian educators that all the words in Scripture are God's words and to disbelieve or disobey any word of it is to disbelieve or disobey God. Our commitment must be to correctly interpret, explain, and apply God's Word, revealing its relevance to all people in every age and in every culture. To that end, we must understand, as Christian educators, that our search for big ideas must start and end with Scripture.

Framing Big Ideas from God's Word

Hadden Robinson (2001) explains that every biblical message or lesson should include interpretation, explanation, and application of a single dominant idea supported by other ideas, all drawn from one passage or several passages of Scripture. Robinson perceives that ideas are essentially composed of two elements: a subject and a compliment. The subject involves the concepts you want to teach, while the complement completes the subject matter by explaining what it is about (what is its substance?). Think about the subject as a question and the compliment as the answer to that question. If you only have a subject, you will be left with open-ended questions that can't explain anything. On the other hand, compliments without subjects are like drawers without a dresser. When the two merge, an idea is formed. For instance, if your subject is "The essence of the kingdom of God," then turn it into a question, "What is the essence of the kingdom of God?" Answer the question, and you will have your compliment. According to Jesus's parables, the kingdom of God can be compared to a mustard seed, leaven (yeast), treasure hidden in a field, a pearl of great price, etc. Another example of a subject is "The faith of Abraham in the book of Genesis." Transposing this subject into a question, you might say, "How is the faith of Abraham displayed in the book of Genesis?" Answer the question by looking at all the examples in Genesis where Abraham was seen displaying his faith in God. For example, in Genesis 22, we see how Abraham was willing to slaughter his only son in faith and obedience to God.

Part of the challenge for Christian educators is to search the scriptures to find the big ideas (subjects and compliments) that have been laid out by each author and then pull them together to form a unit or course of instruction. That is why Robinson suggests that we begin with a main theme or a problem (referring back to what you learned in chapter 4) and then confer with passages that relate to that topic by studying the context. Find relevant passages by consulting concordances, topical Bibles, or the indexes inside theology books. These will direct you to discussions of the subject matter and/or passages of Scripture where the idea or doctrine is based. If you are more acquainted with Scripture, you may already have a knowledge base that will accelerate your effort. Either way, as Robinson advises, you may want to read some books that wrestle with moral and ethical issues from a Christian perspective that may not only analyze the problem but also suggest biblical material to be considered.

Once you have gathered together relevant passages, search for the biblical writer's central ideas derived from an exegetical study. One of the best texts that I have read on biblical/exegetical interpretation is *Grasping God's Word* by Duvall and Hays (2001). While the scope of this book does not lend itself to a lengthy discourse on biblical interpretation, I will summarize Duvall and Hays's thesis. They write that there is a river of differences separating us from the biblical audience and to whom the Bible was originally written (e.g., culture, language, time, situations, covenants, etc.). To cross the river of differences, we must grasp the text in their town (by considering what the text meant to the original audience), measure the width of the river (by considering the differences between them and us), cross the principle bridge (by considering the theological principle in the text), and grasp the text in our town (by considering how Christians today should apply the text). Only after understanding the historical/cultural context and literary context of God's Word will we be able to discover the author's central idea and apply it to our lives. The author's central ideas should lend themselves to the development of your big idea statements that will be emphasized in each lesson. These statements should fall in line with your main theme/course description and educational goals.

The other part of the challenge in developing a series of lessons based on a single topic is dealing with several passages that must be examined in their unique context. This will inevitably take more time than studying just one passage. Take for instance one of the examples I used above that dealt with the essence of the Kingdom of God. For this, you may want to exegete Matthew 13:31–35, as this passage describes how Jesus compared the mustard seed and leaven (yeast) to the Kingdom of God. Along with this, it would be helpful to study his stories of the treasure and the pearl of great price from later in that chapter, verses 44–46. These are just a few of Jesus's many parables about the Kingdom of God. The challenge is to not just rush through passages such as these. Instead, study them in their context so you will glean a more thorough understanding.

Moreover, we must all fight the urge to want to read something significant into a passage that isn't actually there. Robinson (2001) warns of this danger by stating that our eagerness to say something helpful to hurting people may end up in a misuse of the Bible (putting words in God's mouth). Don't fall for the trap of stating a message that the biblical authors never intended. Don't come to a text with the intent of trying to prove a point. For instance, I have heard many pastors and Christian leaders alike contextualize and misuse the meaning Proverbs 29:18 (NIV), which states, "Where there is no revelation, people cast off restraint; but blessed is the one who heeds wisdom's instruction." The word for revelation here is often translated vision, which in turn has led many people to use this passage in an effort to set goals for a Christian organization or to "dream cast." However, as Ross (1991) correctly delineates, this Scripture has little to do with our modern understanding and definition of vision. Instead, it refers to divine communication to the prophets (God's Word). Ross concludes that people should expect spiritual and political anarchy when no revelation from God is present. In other words, where God's Word is not available or valued, people will become spiritually and politically bankrupt. Thankfully, the writer of this proverb closes with a caveat about the above warning. He uses the warning to lead believers to the second phrase in the verse, which affirms that the one who obeys God's instruction is blessed. As Robinson suggests, we must allow a passage to speak for itself by setting it in its greater framework. We can do this by looking at commentaries that discuss why a book was written and by examining an outlining of its contents.

Richards and Bredfeldt (1998) further this discussion by bringing to light two questions that Christian educators must answer when considering what their big ideas (or aims) will be: What do I want the student to learn (the exegetical idea)? How do I want the student to change (the pedagogical idea)? The authors state, "Creative Bible teachers focus on helping learners bridge the gaps between the world of the Bible and the world of the student" (p. 132). This means that after teachers grasp the transferable concept from Scripture, they must be able to develop the pedagogical idea (how the information will be presented to students). Wiggins and McTighte (2005) pick up on this notion when they state that big ideas are not big solely because of their intellectual scope but also because of their pedagogical power. They are "conceptual tools for sharpening thinking, connecting discrepant pieces of knowledge, and equipping learners for transferable applications" (p. 70). This should signify to us that big ideas assist learners in making sense of prior learning and making foreign ideas seem more recognizable.

The Sequence of Instruction

Now that you have a basic idea of the pieces of content you will be sharing with your students, you will need to decide the order in which you will present each concept or big idea. Which piece of the puzzle should come first or go last? The first stage of this process is to "decompose" the task or break it down into its most basic components. This involves identifying what students will need to do in order to attain your educational goals (Smith and Ragan, 2005). In other words, consider the steps someone must go through in order to accomplish the learning task.

It may be helpful to look at decomposing learning tasks like learning how to prepare a meal. For instance, think about what it takes to make spaghetti with homemade tomato and meat sauce. Before you ever start cooking, you need to know how to use a stove with pots and pans. You also need to know how to measure ingredients and read a recipe. These are prerequisites. What would happen if you couldn't decode an abbreviation or if you didn't know which pans to use? You would probably be lost right out of the gate. After attaining the proper prerequisite information, your goal will be twofold: to be able to cook the sauce to perfection, and to be able to prepare the noodles. But doing this will take another level of understanding. First of all, you have to know how to cook meat, make the sauce (using your ability to read a recipe and measure the proper ingredients), and then mix them together. Concurrently, you will have to boil water, cook the noodles in the water (for an appropriate amount of time), and then drain the excess water from them. The only thing remaining is to place the sauce on top of the cooked noodles, and then you are ready to eat! Look at figure 5 and consider the steps it takes to accomplish the goal of making spaghetti with homemade tomato and meat sauce.

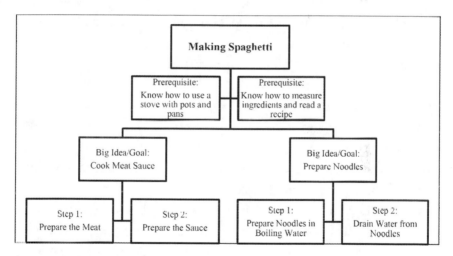

Figure 5: Sequencing Illustration

Let me share another example of decomposing learning tasks, this time from a theology unit investigating the doctrine of bibliology (the study of the Bible). Before beginning this particular unit, students should have taken Old Testament and New Testament Survey courses. These prerequisites will give learners a background in biblical studies that will be needed in order to succeed in systematic theology units.

There are three educational goals for this unit on bibliology. The first goal is for students to know the reasons why the Bible is relevant in today's culture. In order to reach this goal, students will need to be taught about the authority of Scripture. This involves the notion that all the words in the Bible are God's words; to disbelieve or disobey any word of Scripture is to disbelieve or disobey God. Because it is authoritative, God's Word is also valid and reliable for all people today. After grappling with this, students will then be exposed to the inerrancy of Scripture. Inerrancy involves the belief that the original manuscripts of the Bible did not contain any errors. Along with this, students will come to know that the Bible is clear, understandable, and a necessity for the lives of Christians.

The second goal for this unit is for students to understand how Scripture was written and passed down through the generations. This goal will be reached, first of all, by discussing how God has revealed himself through general and specific revelation. General revelation includes the mountains, the stars, and the entire universe that declares his majesty. Specific revelation involves the words of the Bible that he gave to its authors. Additionally, this section will deal with the canon of the Bible. Students will learn the difference between canonical and non-canonical books. Along with this, they will discover the strict guidelines that people used to determine if a book should be considered canonical. Lastly, the class will discuss modern translations of the Bible.

Lastly, the third goal for this bibliology unit is for students to be able to demonstrate that they can effectively interpret and apply a passage of Scripture. To accomplish this goal, students will first learn how important it is to thoroughly observe what the Scripture says. This will involve gaining an understanding of the literary context of a passage. After this, students will learn how to gain knowledge about the Bible's historical/cultural context. This involves a study of the biblical writer, biblical audience, and any other background elements that are deemed helpful (e.g., social customs, religious customs, political happenings, or economic realities). Once this is accomplished, students will turn their attention to applying the passage to their personal lives. Application involves the response of the reader to the author's meaning communicated in the text.

Figure 6 gives a representation of the learning tasks involved in this bibliology unit.

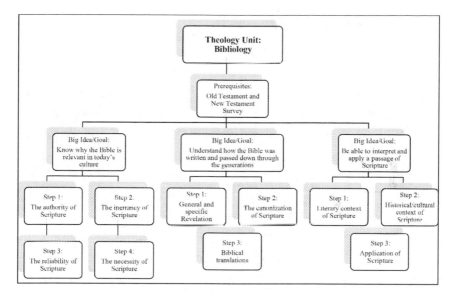

Figure 6: Sequencing Unit on Bibliology

    The key to this process is in understanding that new learning is built on the back of previous learning. How does your lesson fit into what is already known? Master teachers are able to make connections and build bridges between what students already know and what they need to know. That is why it is essential to consider what prerequisite information students need to have before beginning your unit of instruction. To determine what prerequisites will be required for your course, break the content down into chunks and ask yourself, "What must the learner know or be able to do to achieve the next step?" Continue to ask this question until each step has been broken down into everything students will need to know in order to achieve each educational goal (Smith and Ragan, 2005). It is from these chunks or steps that you will develop instructional objectives that I will discuss in the next chapter. For now, follow Gunter, Estes, and Mintz's (2007) suggestions when it comes to ordering subject matter.

They propose organizing content or the written curriculum through a chronological approach or thematic approach.

The Chronological Approach

The easiest and perhaps most obvious way to group educational goals and lesson content is to place them in chronological order. Historical events line up chronologically, and you can teach about biblical dates and/or biblical characters in this fashion. If you wanted to teach a class about the history of the kings of Israel up through the division of the kingdom of Israel, you would probably want to choose this approach. Your educational goals would most likely be set up in the cognitive domain, and you would focus on factual knowledge while challenging your students to be able to remember certain facts about the lives of Saul, David, Solomon, Rahoboam, and Jeroboam (listed in chronological order). This approach may also be useful if you are teaching through books of the Bible. In that case, you would want to organize your educational goals and content in order by the natural literary divisions and outline of the book.

The Thematic Approach

Rather that teaching chronologically, many educational ministers choose to organize their lessons thematically in order to bring together various topics. Teachers can do this by making discriminations within the content. This is when you differentiate (or use comparisons and contrasts) between two or more people, themes, or doctrines. For instance, think about how David's life was different and/or similar to Saul's and Solomon's lives. A series involving these three characters will elaborate on each individual separately and then consider their numerous traits collectively. You can then challenge your students to consider if they are more like David, Saul, or Solomon. It may also help to utilize a Venn diagram to organize your thoughts in this process. Figure 7 gives an example of this by deciphering major themes in Galatians and Romans. In this example, you would teach through each book looking at its main themes and then compare the two so students will understand how they are distinct and yet similar. Moreover, if you are teaching a class involving skills, you may want to consider organizing your lessons moving from simple to complex. Think about this like you were teaching algebra. If you want students to learn how to solve equations, you will have to begin with the basics (i.e., addition, subtraction, multiplication, and division). Then you can move on to order of operations and solving for variables. Similarly, if you are teaching a basic hermeneutical skills class, begin with having students observe the text, then move on to literary context and historical/cultural context, before landing on application.

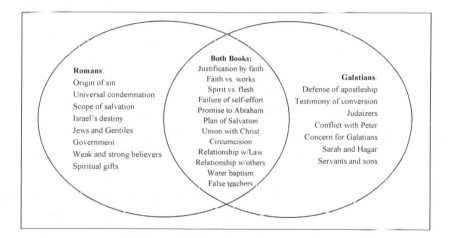

Figure 7: Venn Diagram Representing Doctrinal Emphasis in Galatians and Romans

Taking all this into consideration, Gunter, Estes, and Mintz suggest that teachers should always ensure that there is a logical order for the sequence of our instruction. Moreover, they need to make obvious connections between the parts to be learned and those already known by the students.

Conclusion

Hadden Robinson (2001) reminds us, "An old recipe for a rabbit stew starts out, 'first catch the rabbit.' That puts first things first. Without the rabbit, there is no dish" (p. 29). I think this is a perfect illustration for understanding the importance of instructional analysis. If we do not put in the necessary time that is needed to figure out who our learners are, what context they will be learning in, what their educational needs are, what the main theme and educational goals will be, and what the scope and the sequence of the content will be, then we will be starting off on the wrong foot. Put the first things first before moving on to lesson planning.

In this chapter, you learned about the final piece of instructional or front-end analysis: the scope and sequence of your content. In order to determine what should be included in your instruction, think about what you need to teach during the course of your unit to prepare your students for the summative assessments. It will help to decompose the learning tasks to figure out what steps are necessary for success. This will also help you sequence your material, and it will help you determine if your students will need prerequisite skills or knowledge in order to succeed in your class. The final chapters of this book will dive into the narrowest part of the instructional design funnel and discuss what goes into individual lesson planning. This includes the development of instructional objectives, teaching strategies, and assessments.

Practice Makes Perfect

Scope and Sequence Worksheet

Directions: Put into practice the concepts you learned from chapters 4–5. Read through Luke 11:1–13 and answer the following questions based on your own educational ministry context.

- If you were to develop a series of lessons based on this passage, what would your main theme be? Write it out in 4–5 sentences.

- Based on your main theme, develop at least two essential questions that need to be answered. Then come up with at least two educational goals tied to a specific learning domain.

- Then consider how you would verify whether or not your students achieved your educational goals through a summative assessment.

- As you break down your topic into its most basic components, think about at least two topics about prayer that you can develop into lessons.

Sources

Duvall, J. S., and J. D. Hays. *Grasping God's Word: A Hands on Approach to Reading, Interpreting, and Applying the Bible.* Grand Rapids, Michigan: Zondervan, 2001.

Gunter, M. A., T. H. Estes, and S. L. Mintz. *Instruction: A Models Approach.* 5th ed. Boston, Massachusetts: Pearson, 2007.

Ledford, B., and P. J. Sleeman. *Instructional Design: System Strategies.* Greenwich, Connecticut: IAP, 2002.

Richards, L. O., and G. O. Bredfeldt. *Creative Bible Teaching.* Chicago, Illinois: Moody Bible Institute, 1998.

Robinson, H. *Biblical Preaching: The Development and Delivery of Expository Messages.* 2nd ed. Grand Rapids, Michigan: Baker Academic, 2001.

Ross, A. P. "Proverbs." In *The Expositor's Bible Commentary: With the New International Version: Vol. 5. Psalms, Proverbs, Ecclesiastes, Song of Songs*, edited by F. E. Gaebelein. Grand Rapids, Michigan: Zondervan, 1991.

Schultz, T., and J. Schultz. *Why Nobody Learns Much of Anything at Church: And How to Fix it.* Loveland, Colorado: Group Publishing, 1993.

Smith, P. L., and T. J. Ragan. *Instructional Design.* 3rd ed. Upper Saddle River, New Jersey: Wiley & Sons, Inc., 2005.

Wiggins, G., and J. McTighte. *Understanding by Design.* 2nd ed. Alexandria, Virginia: ASCD, 2005.

Willhite, K., and S. M. Gibson. *The Big Idea of Biblical Preaching: Connecting the Bible to People.* Grand Rapids, Michigan: Baker Academic, 2003.

PART II

INSTRUCTIONAL STRATEGY

Objectives for Chapters 6-8

By the end of this section, you will be able to:

- Create instructional objectives and learning targets for each lesson you will teach.
- Select appropriate teaching strategies to help students reach educational goals.
- Choose appropriate teaching resources.
- Come up with a variety of formative assessments to keep students on track.
- Give helpful feedback to students.

You have analyzed your learners and the learning context. You have conducted a needs assessment and determined your main theme, essential questions, and educational goals. You have established the scope of content that you wish to project to your students and sequenced it in a way that will make the most sense to your specific learners. In short, you have conquered the instructional or front-end analysis of your instructional design. However, your job is not complete. In fact, you are just getting warming up. It's now time to plan for each lesson and execute that plan in your specific educational ministry.

The next few chapters will investigate the final three phases of preparation, which involve individual lesson planning (the micro level of instructional design). Below is a generic outline of what should be included in each lesson plan. You will notice that the first three aspects of your lesson plan have already been generated from your instructional analysis. The remaining four areas will be discussed in Part II of this book (instructional strategy).

- *Title/Big idea*: Give your lesson a title and explain the big idea that undergirds the content.
- *Educational goal*: Which educational goal is this lesson meant to fulfill?
- *Lesson context*: Who is involved? How much time will be allotted? Where will the lesson take place?
- *Instructional objectives*: What do you want students to know as a result of this lesson, and how will you expect them to display their knowledge? This must be measurable behavior and should be written with an action verb.
- *Detailed lesson procedures/content to be presented*: This includes the way that an instructional objective will be taught. What teaching strategies will you utilize and how will your content be structured?
- *Resources*: Are there any additional resources you will utilize for your lesson? (e.g., PowerPoint, handouts, videos, books, articles, etc.)
- *Assessments and reinforcements (feedback)*: How will students put your material into practice? How will you verify their achievements in both formative and summative contexts? What will you communicate to students to help them improve in the learning process?

6

ARRANGE INSTRUCTIONAL OBJECTIVES

Hendricks, I've been preaching for twelve years without an objective, and it finally dawned on me one day that if I didn't know what I was doing, there was a good possibility that they didn't know what they were supposed to do. So I've started coming into the pulpit with clear-cut objectives.

—Howard Hendricks

Pray for us, too, that God may open a door for our message, so that we may proclaim the mystery of Christ, for which I am in chains. Pray that I may proclaim it clearly, as I should.

—Colossians 4:3–4 (NIV)

While attending Denver Seminary, I took a theological methods course. This course was designed to help pastors and teachers explore the various approaches people take when it comes to the formation and function of theology in their lives. After attending all the classes, reading the required textbooks, and writing the necessary research papers, the final assessment was to be an exam based on the material given in class. Before the test, some of my classmates asked the professor what we should study, and his reply was that we should study everything. So in preparation for the exam, I reviewed my textbooks and studied the notes I had accumulated over the course of the semester. I ended up memorizing the information I deemed to be important, which made me feel very confident that I would pass with flying colors. However, when I came to class the next day, my jaw dropped as I realized that much of the information I had studied was not on the test. I wondered how I could have missed what was most important to my professor.

Unfortunately, this is a problem that students face more often than we'd like to admit. As teachers, we believe that everything we share with students is important, and we want them to learn it all. However, students can only write so fast and only remember so much. That is why students tend to ask which parts of each lesson are most important and what they will be expected to understand for upcoming assessments. Perhaps the most effective way to communicate this to students is through instructional objectives (stated as learning targets as I will discuss later in this chapter). Objectives/learning targets inform students of the key pieces of information they should be looking for and are trying to comprehend in your lessons. They also prepare students for what they will be expected to do to show you they have learned the material. Robert Mager (1997) claims that when teachers fail to communicate their objectives to students or fail to make connections between their objectives and test items, they produce learners who have no idea what they are learning or why they are learning it. He goes on to explain that unless objectives are clearly and firmly fixed in the minds of both teachers and students, their tests are likely to be "at best, misleading; at worst, they will be irrelevant, unfair, or uninformative" (p. 15).

In the last chapter, you learned how to decompose your educational goal into steps or processes. Now in this next phase of your instructional design, you will turn each of those steps into instructional objectives. As Ledford and Sleeman (2002) indicate, educational goals are reached through the achievement of instructional objectives. Instructional objectives include statements of performance that specify the intended or terminal behavior, the conditions where the behavior will occur, and the standard or acceptable level at which the learner will demonstrate the behavior. In this way, your objectives should naturally branch off from your educational goals.

Let me quickly reiterate what I mentioned in chapter 4 about the differences between educational goals and instructional objectives. Your goals will be more general and less precise than your objectives. **Instructional objectives** then are specific phrases that include a collection of words and/or pictures intended to display exactly what students will be expected to do as a result of instruction. In his book, *Preparing Instructional Objectives: A Critical Tool in the Development of Effective Instruction*, Robert Mager (1997) states that it is only after teachers are able to clearly specify instructional objectives that they will be able to select and arrange learning experiences for students in accordance with the content at hand. In conjunction with this, objectives prepare teachers to evaluate student performance in accordance with the instructional objectives that have been selected.

While the Bible does not specifically address instructional objectives (as they are a modern-day instructional practice), I do believe we can garner some of the principles of objectives from certain passages of Scripture. Consider, for example, God's instructions to Moses and the Israelites after they were rescued from Egypt. God's desire was for the children of Israel to be set apart from the other nations of the world, and so he had Moses transcribe 613 commandments in the Torah (the first five books of the Bible) that they were to follow. In Deuteronomy 31:12 (NIV), God told Moses, "Assemble the people—men, women and children, and the foreigners residing in your towns—so they can listen and learn to fear the Lord your God and follow carefully all the words of this law." Similarly, in Deuteronomy 4:10 (NIV) Moses reminded the Israelites that God had commanded him to share the decrees of God "so that they may learn to revere me as long as they live in the land and may teach them to their children." God wanted all the Israelites to learn his commandments and learn what it meant to fear him, so that they would respond appropriately. In essence, they were to carefully follow his words and revere him as long as they live. Again, these aren't instructional objectives per se, but the principle that undergirds these words is very similar. God wanted them to learn something and be able to do something in response. That is what instructional objectives are meant to accomplish.

Pulling this all together, this chapter will expose you to the three essential elements that comprise instructional objectives: conditions, performance, and criteria. These three elements are the staples of Robert Mager's research. Additionally, you will learn how to communicate these objectives to your students in the form of *learning targets* that are easier for students to digest. As you read through this chapter, keep in mind that educational goals and objectives are worded in ways that benefit teachers, but learning targets are worded in a way that will benefit students (Moss and Brookhart, 2012).

The Building Blocks of Instructional Objectives

Objectives serve as the basis for what is to be learned, how well it should be performed, and under what conditions it will be performed. This underlies Mager's highly esteemed three-point method for creating instructional objectives—an objective statement that includes conditions, performance, and criteria (the CPC method). *Conditions* involve the situations under which a student's performance will occur. The *performance* aspect states what a learner will be expected to be able to do and/or produce to be considered competent. The last piece, *criteria*, describes acceptable performance or how well someone would have to perform to be considered competent (see table 4). It should be noted that these three aspects of objectives do not need to be written in a specific order.

Mager's Three Point Instructional Objectives		
Conditions	Performance	Criteria
Identifies the tools, materials, aids, or facilities to be used in performing the task or assessment.	Involves observable action that students will be able to complete during evaluation (combines a verb the action that's expected).	Defines what the acceptable level of performance will be.
Informs students of what they will have (or not have) to work with when performing.	Dependent on cognitive, behavioral, or affective goals or outcomes.	Given in terms of quantity, quality, or time (speed)
Describes the real world conditions under which the performance will occur.	Helps students take ownership of what they are learning.	Provides teachers with a standard in which to judge success, and students with details of how "good is good enough."

Table 4: Mager's Three-Point Instructional Objectives

Conditions of Performance

In every objective, you should describe the actual conditions under which a student will be required to perform the learning task or upcoming assessment (formative or summative). Identify what tools, materials, aids, or facilities that will be used in performing the task or assessment. Examples of such phrases would include: "without a biblical concordance " or "by checking biblical maps." Mager adds that in order to avoid any unnecessary student surprises, teachers should state the main intent of the objective and describe the main conditions under which the performance will occur. For example, "Be able to saw a two-by-two piece of wood" is different from "Given a circular saw, be able to saw a two-by-two piece of wood." If your students were expecting a handsaw but were given a circular saw they had never used before, then they might be in trouble.

That is why conditions of performance are important. You can avoid miscommunications by adding relevant conditions that may impact the student's performance. Tell your students what they will have (or not have) to work with when performing, and tell them of any special circumstances that will affect their performance. Mager offers several questions that you can ask yourself when trying to identify conditions. They are below.

- What will the learner be expected to use when performing (e.g., tools, forms, etc.)?

- What will the learner not be allowed to use while performing (e.g., checklists or other aids)?
- What will be the real-world conditions under which the performance will be expected to occur (e.g., a mission trip, couple's retreat, in front of an audience, at home alone)?

Actual Performance

This is the observable action. What is it that you want your students to be able to do to show they have learned what you wanted them to? The performance you select may be dependent on whether you desire cognitive, behavioral, affective goals or outcomes. Larry Lindquist (2010), a professor at Denver Seminary, recommends utilizing case specific verbs for all three of these outcomes. They are listed below.

- *Cognitive* (learn, know, understand, memorize, recite, create, describe, define)
- *Behavioral* (build, create, journal, help, serve, assist, disassemble, assemble, list)
- *Affective* (appreciate, enjoy, embrace, have a deeper love for, fear, hate, create a deeper desire for)

This list is an enhancement of the micro level verbs from Bloom's Taxonomy that were discussed in chapter 4. The performance aspect of your instructional objective should combine your verb with the action you expect out of your students. For example,

- students will be able to *create* a spiritual journal;
- students will *recite* John 3:16–17;
- students will *interview* someone with a different religion;
- students will *produce* a report.

In sum, performance is described by a "doing" word. If it describes something that you expect your students to be able to do, then it is a performance. However, if your statement only includes something they can be (e.g., students will be knowledgeable about), then it is not a performance. Words involving actions like *running, solving, writing* are doing words, but *happy, understanding, appreciating* are not. As Mager (1997) surmises, students will generally best remember what they understand, and they will understand the things that they think about and apply. In this way, they begin to take ownership of their own learning.

Measurable Criteria for the Performance

What will you consider as acceptable performance? Will this be in terms of quantity (how many), quality (how well), or time (how fast)? It is important for students to know how well they have to perform in order to be considered competent. Mager lays out several advantages of using certain criteria such as these. First of all, teachers will have a standard in which to judge the success of their instruction. Secondly, students will know how to tell when they have met or even exceeded the teacher's expectations. Thirdly, teachers will have the basis for proving that their students can do what they set out for them to do in the first place.

Let's look more specifically at the different kinds of criteria. When it comes to time (or speed), consider whether or not you want them to have a time limit to show you they can perform the learning task. Time limits on tests tell students how long they have to complete the questions. If you want them to answer essay questions on an exam, how much time will be allotted? If you want them to complete a project, will you give them two weeks or two months? An example of a criteria involving speed might be: "Given a Bible in their hands, students will be able to locate verses containing four types of biblical genres within ten minutes." Without the speed criteria, they could take all day or all week to complete that objective.

Objectives dealing directly with quality (or accuracy) focus primarily on how precise students need to be. Will you require your students to simply find the biblical book that contains the genera of poetry, or will they have to find an exact verse? Will you require all the students to score at least an eighty percent on a test before moving on to the next concept? Do students have to perform a task appropriately in order to get credit? Let me give you an example: "Without having to refer to their Bibles, students will be able to recite 2 Timothy 3:1–17 with no more than three errors." Whatever the measurable criteria you are looking for, make sure that it reflects a realistic expectation. Don't require every student to receive a one hundred percent just to pass the class. That wouldn't be very realistic, and frankly, it would breed anxiety.

The third type of criteria—quantity—hedges on an amount or a size that you want to include in an assignment or assessment. Do you want students to come up with at least five observations about the differences between Saul and David's leadership? Will you require students to create a poem that is at least fifteen lines long? An example of an instructional objective with criteria that focuses on quantity would state, "Utilizing the church's library resources, students will be able to produce a two-to-three-page essay (typed) concerning the differences between Christianity and Buddhism." Without an exact designation, students may end up writing an essay that is too short or too long. This takes the guessing work out of the equation.

Transform Instructional Objectives into Learning Targets

Gardner (1983) asserts that communicating objectives to students will help eliminate potential conflicts, contradictions, or misunderstandings about the material being presented. That's great in theory, but the honest truth is that instructional objectives are useful mainly for teachers. They are often written in ways that are too overbearing for students. In fact, if you were the student, would you want to memorize an objective that speaks of you in the third person (i.e., "The student will—")?

In its place, Moss and Brookhart (2012) encourages teachers to restate instructional objectives in terms of learning targets. These are more palatable for students to digest. While educational goals and instructional objectives are written for the teacher's benefit, learning targets are written for the student's benefit. Moss and Brookhart define **learning targets** as statements that describe what students will learn and do during a particular lesson. This includes the lesson-sized chunk of learning you expect your students to know. The important thing is to make sure that your targets express, from the student's point of view, what knowledge or skills they will need in order to succeed. Use student-friendly language that students will be able to understand. This includes simple words and short sentences. Instead of saying, "The student will," use first person *we* or *I* to communicate that they are the ones doing the learning.

As Moss and Brookhart delineate, learning targets speak to students, express the essentials of the lesson, and provide students a rationale for why and what you are asking them to do is important. To get a better grasp on this concept, consider applying these author's four steps for creating and communicating learning targets.

- Step 1: Explain the learning target in student-friendly, developmentally appropriate terms. (We are learning to …)
- Step 2: Describe the performance of understanding. (We will show that we can do this by …)
- Step 3: Make it relevant so they understand why it is important. Is this a skill or knowledge they will need in the future? (It is important for us to learn this because …)
- Step 4 (optional): Describe what the students should be looing for. (To know how well we are learning this, we will look for …)

Let me give you an example of an instructional objective and its learning target based on a biblical interpretation course I teach. In one of my lessons, I explain the four steps or procedures for determining application from the biblical text based partly on the book *Introduction to Biblical Interpretation* by Klein, Blomberg, and Hubbard Jr.: 1.) discover the "intended response" which the biblical author expected the original readers to make; 2.) note any implied "cross-cultural principles" for Christian living; 3.) establish how individual Christians today can apply the theological principles in their lives; 4.) consider several tests of validity for the application that was found (Is it universally true for all believers? Is it supported by theological, not cultural arguments? Is it contrary to the expressed will of God?). Based on the above content, an instructional objective may be, "Students will be able to implement all four procedures for determining application from God's Word appropriately when studying 1 Corinthians 9:7–12a." Transforming this into a learning target, I would tell students, "Today, our learning target is to learn four procedures for applying God's Word to our lives and be able to use each procedure accurately when studying 1 Corinthians 9:7–12a. This will prepare us to correctly apply any portion of Scripture we are studying."

Conclusion

Before I close this chapter, I want to clarify that every lesson will have instructional objectives, but that doesn't mean that you will only have one. The educational goal that you decomposed in chapter 5 helped you bring focus to the steps or processes that are needed in order to reach that goal. However, each step might have two or three objectives tied to it. Sometimes, your lesson will only have one objective, but other times, you will have more. It will depend on size of the chunk of learning you are trying to get across on a particular day. Moreover, you may have the same objective for several lessons if you are spending more time in a content area.

That being said, I want to encourage you to take the time to think through the conditions, performances, and levels of criteria you will be exhibiting through your instructional objectives. I have seen many teachers skip past this because they don't think that really thinking this through will make that much of a difference, but I think it does. Furthermore, think through how you will communicate those objectives to your students. I appreciate Moss and Brookhart's model of learning targets because it explains objectives in a way that students can understand. I have always had great feedback from my students in regard to learning targets. Believe it or not, students relish the opportunity to get a sneak peak at the lesson because it helps them gear their minds to what is important; what they should be looking for in your lesson. In the next two chapters, you will take all the information you have learned so far in this book and let it govern the learning experiences you will bring to the table in your educational ministry context. How will you structure your lessons? What are some creative ways that can you present material? How will you assess that students really learned the material you presented?

Practice Makes Perfect

Instructional Objectives Worksheet

Directions: Read through the following list of instructional objectives and determine which of them correctly incorporate conditions, performance, and criteria by placing checks in the appropriate blanks to the side. Make corrections to any inaccurate objectives, and then turn them into learning targets written from a student's point of view (adapted from Mager, 1997).

	Conditions	Performance	Criteria
1.) Students will have a thorough understanding of the doctrine of justification.	_____	_____	_____
2.) Students will be able to demonstrate their empathy for the underprivileged in the community.	_____	_____	_____
3.) Students will be able to defend the doctrine of the Trinity through an oral exam, citing at least three Old Testament and three New Testament Passages.	_____	_____	_____
4.) Students will appreciate the importance of giving of their time, talent, and treasure.	_____	_____	_____
5.) Students will know how to correctly interpret a passage of Scripture.	_____	_____	_____

6.) Without memory aids
   or other assistance,
   students will demonstrate
   a knowledge of the
   principles of biblical
   application.   _____   _____   _____

7.) Without reference
   materials, students will
   be able to describe the
   three main themes of the
   book of John in a five
   paragraph essay.   _____   _____   _____

Sources

Ledford, B. R., and P. J. Sleeman. *Instructional Design: System Strategies.* Greenwich, Connecticut: IAP, 2002.

Lindquist, L. *Writing Goals and Indicators.* [class handout]. Littleton, Colorado: Denver Seminary, 2010.

Mager, R. F. *Preparing Instructional Objectives: A Critical Tool in the Development of Effective Instruction.* 3rd ed. Atlanta, Georgia: Center for Effective Performance, 1997.

Moss, C. M., and S. M. Brookhart. *Learning Targets: Helping Students Aim for Understanding in Today's Lesson.* Alexandria, Virginia: ASCD, 2012.

Gardner, H. *Frames of Mind: The Theory of Multiple Intelligences.* New York, New York: Basic Books, 1983.

Duvall, J. S., and J. D. Hays. *Grasping God's Word: A Hands on Approach to Reading, Interpreting, and Applying the Bible.* Grand Rapids, Michigan: Zondervan, 2001.

7

SELECT APPROPRIATE
TEACHING STRATEGIES

*Highly effective teachers design better learning experiences for
their students in part because they conceive of teaching as fostering
learning. Everything they do stems from their strong concern
for and understanding of the development of their students.
They follow few traditions blindly and recognize when change
in the conventional course is both necessary and possible.*

—Ken Bain

*Let my teaching fall like rain and my words descend
like dew, like showers on new grass,
like abundant rain on tender plants.*

—Deuteronomy 32:2 (NIV)

When I was in high school, I had the opportunity to attend the
Emmy award-winning production *Blast!* This spectacle ingeniously
joined brass and percussion instrumentalists with an ensemble of
singers and dancers. The cast presented what can only be described as
a musical celebration that bridged rock 'n' roll, jazz, blues, and classical
music. As a budding musician, I remember feeling mesmerized as
this innovative marching band and choreographed color guard moved

around the stage with such precision and class. Their commitment to artistic creativity and excellence was infectious, and it made me want to pursue the same kind of excellence in every area of my life.

Whenever I reflect on my experience that day, I cannot help but be reminded of what Cliff Schimmels (1999) wrote about the potential of the classroom experience. He claimed that being a part of a good lesson can be like watching an orchestra when all the instruments are harmonizing and creating a unified melody. If you were to take a step back and assess your educational ministry at this moment, would you say that this is what you see on a regular basis? Do you see yourself orchestrating a grand symphony in your particular context? If not, what can you do better to conduct or direct your students? How can you become more creative in your teaching style? I believe part of the answer involves broadening your teaching strategy toolbox, or as Gardner (1983) puts it, "cast the net more widely." Classes will be more apt to form a perfect melody when teachers diversify their teaching methods, allowing students to become more engaged. As one of my former professors used to say, the larger your repertoire of teaching styles, the better your students will be accommodated, and the more successful they will be. Moreover, the better suited we will be to reach out to diverse populations.

This is something we can learn from Jesus's approach to education that is on display in the gospels. People came in large numbers to see and hear from Jesus, and as Matthew 7:28 (NIV) expresses, "When Jesus had finished saying these things, the crowds were amazed at his teaching." I believe this was not only due to his content but also his engaging teaching strategies or pedagogy. As Keith Ferdinando (2013) suggests, Jesus's pedagogy merits attention from anybody engaged in the spiritual formation of Christian believers. His ability to diversify his teaching methods should inspire us to reassess our current values, pedagogies, and structures in our own educational ministry contexts. Although Jesus is seen at times teaching more formally (as in the Sermon on the Mount in Matthew 5–7), Ferdinando brings to light the fact that Jesus often fostered an atmosphere which expected and even welcomed questions, discussion, and debate. Not only did he seek to impart truth through his monologues, but he also sought to engage their intelligence and make them wrestle with the contemporary concerns of the day. Jesus's use of parables shows his concern for communicating spiritual truths in ways that were culturally familiar to the masses, but yet he expected them to make both a mental and spiritual effort to grasp the deeper levels of meaning. Ferdinando goes on to say that they had to "become part of the story and find their own place within it" (p. 367). In sum, Jesus wanted his disciples and the crowds that gathered around him to become active in their learning and engage him in discussion about various relevant issues. In today's terminology, we call this active learning.

Likewise, today's Christian educators should strive for engagement and active learning in their educational ministry context. As mentioned above, teachers should broaden their teaching strategy toolbox in order to reach diverse populations. However, many Christian educators have a tendency to teach one way, which is often the way they personally like to be taught. But that is not necessary the way their learners need to be taught. That is why it is important for teachers to know the learning styles of their students. In fact, lesson plans should be a by-product of what teachers know about their students. So once you have completed the groundwork required to understand your target audience and their needs, turn your attention to the various teaching methods and strategies available for achieving the learning task.

A good teaching strategy will involve more than just activities. Teachers are responsible for developing the procedures and strategies for how they will present the content, motivate students, and help those students learn the material (Dick, Carey, and Carey, 2009, p. 165). In order to do so, Smith and Ragan (2005) propose that teachers first develop an **organizational strategy** that will help them sequence the chosen content that is to be presented and determine how that content will be presented. This is the overall framework of the lesson and how the lesson is organized. Additionally, a **delivery strategy** must be fleshed out that will help teachers determine what instructional mediums will be used. Will you use cooperative learning groups, drill and practice, reflective discussions, group presentations, debates, graphic organizers, etc.? Along with this, will you incorporate PowerPoint slides, handouts, movie clips, music, self-assessments, art, etc.?

This chapter will investigate these concepts and give you practical ways to incorporate them into your educational ministry. I will also expose you to several lesson-planning models that you can adapt for your classes. After this, I will outline several types of teaching strategies that you can incorporate into your lessons and assignments. This includes cooperative learning strategies, nonlinguistic representation strategies, and traditional linguistic strategies. Lastly, I will close with several suggestions for choosing appropriate strategies for your lessons. While the goal is not to have a perfect lesson, you should strive to find the right way to teach the ideas or skills you want your learners to integrate into their lives.

Developing an Organizational Strategy

What will the overall framework of your lesson look like? How will you sequence your content? How will you present it? To begin answering these questions, Smith and Ragan (2005) suggest looking at what psychologists believe happens cognitively to students when they learn. In other words, we need to examine the cognitive processes or mental activities that occur in the minds of students during a lesson. Your organizational strategy should facilitate these mental operations.

In his book, *Learning Theories: An Educational Perspective*, Dale Schunk (2012) refers to this progression as information processing. Schunk explains that if our goal as teachers is to help students transfer information from their short-term memories to their long-term memories, we need to understand how students take in, process, and store information. For starters, students take in information that is related to the learning task through their sensory registers (e.g., sounds, sights, odors, tastes, etc.). This is what psychologists refer to as attention. Because our attention capabilities are limited, we are only able to attend to a few things at a time. So students must find a way to ignore competing stimuli (any distraction that would keep them from learning). As students attach meaning to the inputs they receive through the senses, they relate new information to old information or make associations. When this happens, they are able to store the new information in their working memory, where they will "use it or lose it." Stated somewhat differently, if we don't do something with what we are learning, we will forget it. That is why students must process what they learn through meaningful rehearsal techniques (e.g., graphic organizers, mnemonics, student activities). The key word in this is *meaningful*. If students understand how important something is, they will probably remember it. However, as Schunk points out, not everything will be meaningful to everyone at the same time, but teachers can assist in this process by encouraging students remain active in the learning process rather than passive. This is why I believe Moses commanded the children of Israel in Deuteronomy 6:4 to put the *Shema* on their doorposts and on their foreheads. This was done so they would be active in their learning and have a visual reminder of this important concept: our God is one!

So what are the implications of such research for our learning environments? For starters, we must know that students have to attend to the information through their senses. This happens through a lesson's introduction, as it must include ideas that engage their interest. Then they must connect new material with old material and make sense of it. This happens in the body of a lesson, as teachers drill the main point's home and help students understand the connections. Lastly, students must review information and make life applications. Obviously, this reflects your conclusion. With that said, in educational settings, we can't stop there. We must assess how well students have adopted these ideas and concepts. I will address this in more detail through the next chapter, but for the purpose of this chapter, I want to expose you to several lesson-planning models that may assist you and fill in the blanks as to what should comprise your lesson's introduction, body, and conclusion (see a comparison of these four models in table 5).

Richards and Bredfeldt's HBLT Model

One of the more popular models for lesson planning in Christian education comes from Richards and Bredfeldt (1998) and their book *Creative Bible Teaching*. This work describes the "hook, book, look, took" (HBLT) method. In this model, teachers open their classes with a *hook* that catches their student's attention and exposes a need for instruction. This phase also sets the goal or direction for the class and says something about why students should pay attention to what will be taught. If this does not happen, students will probably tune out. The next element of this model, *book*, challenges teachers to turn to the Bible where they will find the source of the answers they are looking for. Here the teacher will clarify the meaning of the passage being studied so students can understand it. Thirdly, teachers *look* at the implications of the biblical message and helps students pull answer from the Bible. This includes helping the class discover and grasp the relationship of the truth just studied to their daily lives. The last segment of instruction, *took*, involves a response as the teacher encourages students to apply what was taught in the lesson.

Simply put, this method appropriately stresses an introduction (the hook), a body (book and look), and a conclusion (took). It has proved to be helpful for many Christian educators over the years (especially those working with younger students). Unique to this model is the emphasis on biblical study, which is neglected in secular models. That being said, I think it is still beneficial to consider some secular models that touch on additional aspects of learning that are not emphasized as much in the "hook, book, look, took" method.

Bernice McCarthy's 4MAT System

Similar to Richards and Bredfeldt's four-step approach, Bernice McCarthy (2006) developed an organizational strategy based on four quadrants of student learning styles. This is commonly known as the "4MAT System." Earlier in this book, I described the four learning styles that McCarthy believes are represented in every learning environment. For the sake of review, I will go over them again here and describe how each style can be reached through her design. The first group is imaginative learners who need to know the why behind what you are teaching. Why is this subject matter important? How does it connect with what they have learned before? These will be the students in your group who are great at seeing the big picture. They are the ones that learn by sensing, feeling, and watching. Secondly, analytical learners like facts and concepts. They will look to you as their primary source of information and will undoubtedly be assessing the value of what you are communicating while you are still teaching it. The third group is referred to as common sense learners because they want to see if what you taught makes sense in the here and now. Is it workable? Can they solve an issue or problem related to the content? They are very hands on in their approach to learning. Lastly, the fourth group is dynamic learners. They want to know how they will use what they have learned. Their desire is to put their faith in action. Akin to the hearts of entrepreneurs, these learners like to start new things or figure out how to do things in a new way.

Given these four groups of learners, McCarthy developed a four-quadrant organizational strategy, similar to a cycle with four axes. Each of the four quadrants is meant to reach out to a different learning style so that everyone is included. LeFever (2004) reiterates the significance of this scheme by stating that since every learner belongs to one of the four quadrants, we can use this information to build a teaching structure that will hopefully lead to success in our learning environments on a regular basis. In other words, it can be a skeleton on which learning can be hung.

The first quadrant or first part of the lesson should begin with what students already know. Prior learning provides the foundation for the new concepts they will learn. Teachers use this time to gain the attention of students and help them focus. It is also an opportunity to share why this subject matter is important, what gives it meaning. In this way, quadrant one reaches out to those who are more imaginative in nature. The purpose of quadrant two then is to introduce the new facts or concepts that need to be taught on that particular day. Aiming at analytic learners, this phase of learning gives students the new information they need to know. Put another way, they are adding new ideas or concepts to what is already known. The next part of the lesson, quadrant three, reaches out to common sense learners and shows them how these ideas and concepts might be useful in their day-to-day lives. It's not enough for them to know about a particular subject. They need skills and experience in order to put it into practice. With that said, this stage should be very practical in nature, as students apply concepts to their lives and make it useable. Lastly, the fourth quadrant allows room for learners to creatively take what was learned in the lesson and use it outside the learning environment. Here the focus is on dynamic learners who need to find the answer to the questions: What can this become? What possibilities can it create? How can it be adapted or refined? Teachers should find innovative ways to spur them on to action, to challenge them to apply the information in different contexts.

Gagne's Nine Events of Instruction

Another secular model for organizational strategy that I believe can be helpful for Christian educators is Robert Gagne's nine events of instruction. Unlike the other two approaches mentioned above, this model gives a more comprehensive look at some additional activities that should be a part of regular instruction. The nine events are listed below with an explanation for how to use them in a more formal classroom setting (as adapted from the University of Florida's Center for Technology and Training, 2015).

1. *Gaining attention.* Akin to Richards and Bredfeldt's *hook* concept, this event of instruction looks to grab the attention of students so they will be more likely to pay attention to the instructor as he or she presents the material. For this, teachers may want to begin with an icebreaker activity, or share a current news event, or give a case study involving the subject matter. Other options would include sharing pictures

or online videos or even giving leading questions that can perk student interest.

2. *Informing the learner of the objective.* As discussed in the previous chapter, instructional objectives are mostly to be used by teachers, but learning targets can benefit students as they are worded in student-friendly, developmentally appropriate terms. Teachers need to ensure that students understand each lesson's learning targets so that they can organize their thoughts regarding what they are about to learn. Learning targets can be given through PowerPoint slides, a syllabus, or they may be simply written on the board, but the important thing is to make sure each student knows what to look for in each lesson.

3. *Stimulating recall of prerequisite/previous learning.* Referring back to the idea that students need to relate new information to old information in order to store it in their working memory, this event of instruction helps students recall previous lectures or prior learning that can be integrated with the current topic. This can simply be done by reviewing pertinent information from the last lesson or by discussing questions that may have surfaced since that time.

4. *Presenting stimulus materials (new content).* Similar to Richards and Bredfeldt's *book and look* concepts, this stage of Gagne's design gives teachers the opportunity to effectively present the current lesson to the group. More time will be devoted to how this event is applied in the learning environment later in this chapter.

5. *Providing learning guidance.* In this event of instruction, teachers provide students with instructions for how to complete guided activities that will help them acclimate the new information that was learned. Here it would be useful to give students a rubric for projects or activities so they will know what is expected of them. This will help students avoid frustration when they are completing the work, as they can't read your mind.

6. *Eliciting performance.* This is the point in the lesson when students are given time to apply the knowledge and/or skills they have learned. Sometimes, you may allow students to work in groups; at other times, they need to show effort on their own. Types of performance may include written assignments, lab manuals, etc. This isn't necessarily a formal assessment but rather practice (before an assessment) that allows them to demonstrate whether or not they are accommodating the new content that you have taught.

7. *Providing feedback.* After students have completed their work, give them feedback on those tasks. This will allow them to pinpoint and correct any issues they have in understanding the material. Students get frustrated when they get problems wrong but have no idea where they went wrong in the first place. Teachers can alleviate frustration by showing them not only what needs to improve but also giving an explanation for it.

8. *Assessing performance.* Assessments will be discussed in detail in the next chapter, but for now, it is important to understand that this event of instruction will allow you and your students to see which areas are mastered and which are not mastered. To ensure mastery, assessments are to be completed independently of any outside help.

9. *Enhancing retention and transfer.* This last event of instruction gives students the opportunity to apply the information to differing contexts. Elizabeth Eyre (in her article "Gagne's Nine Levels of Learning: Training Your Team Effectively") echoes this by stating that teachers should allow students to demonstrate understanding by transferring their new knowledge or skill to differing situations other than what they are used to. She goes on to claim that repeated practice helps ensure that people retain information and use it effectively. It is through this process that students can begin to relate course material to their personal lives and move information from their working memories to their long-term memories.

144

Smith and Ragan's Fifteen Steps of Instruction

Not to be outdone by Gagne, Smith and Ragan (2005) take his nine events and turn them into fifteen. While it may seem redundant to explain some of the aspects of instruction already described above, I do want to list and give a brief synopsis of these fifteen steps of instruction, as you may want to add or take away pieces of each approach to construct your own methodology. Smith and Ragan break their activities down into sections that include the introduction, body, and conclusion/assessment.

Introduction:

- *Activate attention to activity.* Gain students' attention and them ready for the lesson.

- *Establish purpose.* Inform the learners of the lesson's purpose.

- *Arouse interest and motivation.* Explain why students should listen to listen to this lesson.

- *Preview learning activity.* Give students an overview of what the lesson will include.

Body:

- *Recall relevant prior knowledge.* Reiterate what students have learned before.

- *Process information and examples.* Present new information and examples.

- *Focus attention.* Informally assess whether or not students are still paying attention to you.

- *Employ learning strategies.* Give directions to students as to how they will practice the new content they have learned.

- *Practice.* Allow students to practice the new content they have learned.

- *Evaluate feedback.* Give feedback to students as to well they accommodated the new content.

Conclusion and Assessment:

- *Summarize and review.* Go back over the main points of the lesson.

- *Transfer learning.* Explain how they will be able to apply new knowledge and skills to a variety of real-life situations and future learning tasks (and preview the next lesson).

- *Remotivate and cease.* Find a way to keep students motivated to continue in their learning of this subject and then close the lesson.

- *Assess learning.* Give a formal assessment to see if students have mastered the content.

- *Evaluate feedback.* Give feedback and provide remediation if necessary.

	HBLT	4MAT	Gagne's Nine Events	Smith and Regan's Fifteen Steps
Introduction	Hook	First Quadrant: Focus on Prior Learning and Meaning	Gain Attention Inform Learner of Objective Stimulate Recall of Previous Learning Present New Content	Activate Attention to Activity Establish Purpose Arouse Interest and Motivation Preview Learning Activity Recall Relevant Prior Knowledge
Body	Book Look	Second Quadrant: Introduce New Concepts Third Quadrant: Give Skills and Experience	Provide Learning Guidance Elicit Performance Provide Feedback	Process Information and Examples Focus Attention Employ Learning Strategies Practice Evaluate Feedback
Conclusion/ Assessment	Took	Fourth Quadrant: Allow Students to Adapt or Refine Content	Assess Performance Enhance Retention and Transfer	Summarize and Review Transfer Learning Re-Motivate and Cease Assess Learning Evaluate Feedback

Table 5: Comparison of Organizational Strategies

These are just several examples of how you can organize or structure your lessons. You may find yourself more comfortable with one style or another, or you may want to develop your own style built on the principles of the ones listed above. Either way, make sure that you take into account the needs of your target audience when developing your lessons. Once you have done this, you will be ready to come up with a delivery strategy that will help you convey material to your students.

Initializing a Delivery Strategy

I have heard it said that the less predictable we are as communicators, the greater our impact will be. Students have a knack for tuning out monotonous lectures, but they will come alive when they are encouraged to participate in their learning. That is why differentiation is so important. The more you vary your teaching strategies and allow your students to engage in what they are learning, the greater of an impression you will make on their lives. They will be more apt to ingest the information you are giving them, and hopefully, that will lead to greater application in their lives. Coley (2012) articulates it this way: "The greater the engagement, the more significant the potential change in the learner, and the deeper the personal meaning will become for him or her" (p. 357). The key word here is *engage*. As Christian educators, we should do everything in our power to help our students engage in the material, because after all, we are teaching the Word of life.

With that said, I do *not* think our pursuit of student engagement should lead us to abandon lecturing in our classes. After all, Jesus often used a lecture style in his ministry. However, he also coupled many of his lectures with other teaching methods that helped his hearers understand his instruction. This insight has led Richards and Bredfeldt (1998) to conclude that when a lecture is accompanied by adequate illustrations, examples, visuals, and stories, it will always be a great method of teaching. They go on to state, "When lecture is developed well and is supported by methods that engage student thinking, it is a powerful means to communicate truth" (p. 194).

In my ministry, I have found **active learning techniques** (ALTs) to be most helpful when it comes to helping students remain engaged in any learning environment. ALTs are modes of teaching that emphasize the importance of active verses passive learning. Educational researcher Ken Bain (2004) states that effective teachers do not rely solely on lectures, not even the highly gifted ones. In fact, he has noticed that the most successful communicators are the ones who look at lectures as a conversation instead of a performance. They interact with students and provide opportunities that allow them to interact with one another and with the material. In this way, everyone in the room can be included. Lectures have a place in this process, but they must be seen as part of a larger quest, one element of a learning environment instead of the whole experience. Bain concludes, "The intention should be to help students understand, not to impress them with the sophistication of the teacher's knowledge" (p. 125). For the rest of this chapter, I will explain in more detail several categories of ALTs that you can include in your educational ministry as you remain faithful to teaching God's Word to his flock and also how to choose which strategies to use in your context. This is where you, as the instructor, can get creative with your content area, and in my opinion, it is where the fun can begin!

Cooperative Learning Strategies

The first category of ALTs includes strategies that maximize the potential of small groups by allowing students to work together to improve everyone's learning. This comes from the understanding that "we learn better together." Marzano, Pickering, and Pollock (2001) add that in **cooperative learning**, students discuss the material with each other, help each other understand it, and encourage each other to work hard. Instead of the teacher being the main communicator of information, these strategies will allow students to discover the content for themselves and interact with it. In this way, the teacher becomes more of a "guide on the side" and only steers them in the right direction. That being said, teachers are still responsible for making several pre-instructional decisions about the content/ materials and who will be included in each group. This includes arranging the room, deciding on the size of the group, assigning students to groups, giving roles to each member of the group, and distributing the materials to each group. While this book does not lend itself toward listing all the dozens of ways cooperative learning is used in learning environments today, let me give you a few strategies that I believe can be useful for any educational ministry context.

Jigsaw Groups

The **jigsaw group** strategy encourages teachers to break down new concepts into segments that students (working in groups) can piece together like a jigsaw puzzle. At first, the teacher will divide the class into groups, and he or she will explain the task and nature of the lesson (including what the criteria will be for success). The task may include questions that need to be answered, or the teacher may have the students read portions of an article or textbook that must be read as part of the whole. Students will then work together in their groups to become "experts" at the section they are responsible for. They will discuss and record their findings. This can be done on a piece of paper or on a dry-erase board. I have even seen some teachers give their students huge pieces of 3M post-it self-stick wall pads that can be written on and hung around the room when completed. While each group is working on their section, the teacher will move around the room to keep them on task, monitor behavior, and answer any questions that arise. When each group is finished with their assigned section, they will present their findings to the whole class, teaching the other groups, and thus completing the "puzzle."

This approach can be particularly useful if your class spends a considerable amount of time examining the lives of biblical characters. In cases like these, you can break up the information or scriptures into a character's early life, ministry exploits, successes/failures, and later/end of life. Consider Jesus's life as an example. You can break the class up into four groups and have the first group look up scriptures about the events surrounding Jesus's birth and ask them questions about those events. A second group can examine his ministry answering questions about that. Thirdly, a group can examine scriptures and questions about the events of his death. Lastly, a fourth group can look up scriptures and answer questions about what Jesus did after he rose again. Then let each group present their conclusions.

The jigsaw group strategy is one of my favorite teaching strategies. I have used it often in both formal classrooms and in church settings. Let me give you an example of how I formatted a class learning about biblical leadership. First of all, I divided the students into four groups. Group 1 was to discuss how leaders delegate. They looked up Exodus 18:7–26 and Acts 6:1–7 to discover lessons about delegation that can be derived from these passages. Group 2 was given the opportunity to discuss how leaders can lead other leaders. They were to read the whole book of Philemon (all twenty-five verses) and discuss what lessons could be learned from the apostle Paul's leadership attitude as he sought to influence Philemon's decision-making process. Group 3 discussed leadership in the home by examining Ephesians 5:21–33, Ephesians 6:1–4, and Deuteronomy 6:4–7. They were asked about what they could learn from these passages about how we should treat one another in the home. Lastly, group 4 had the responsibility to examine leadership in the church. From 1 Timothy 3:13 and Titus 1:6–9, I asked them to come up with a list of characteristics that should be evident in our church's leaders. When every group was finished, they all reported their findings to the rest of the class. We discussed each aspect of leadership together, and I found student engagement skyrocketing as we did this.

Think, Pair, Share

As another variation of collaborative learning groups, the think-pair-share technique calls for students to work in pairs to grapple with the big ideas of a lesson. At first, each student is given a question, problem, or assignment to work on (*think*). Then the teacher will *pair* off each student to discuss the ideas or thoughts that each came up with. They can even use this time to collaborate to delineate a more thorough answer. Then each group will *share* those conclusions with the whole class. The strength of this approach is not only in its simplicity but also in its ability to refine ideas and make arguments stronger. Moreover, as I've heard it said before, students will be more apt to share their ideas with the class as a whole when there is at least one other person in the class who is in agreement about that idea. This is especially a great strategy to utilize if you do not have enough time for jigsaw groups but still want students to interact with each other to build better ideas. Think-pair-share activities usually only involve one or two questions that can be answered in a short amount of time, while jigsaw groups will usually take more time, energy, and effort. Additionally, jigsaw groups require that groups work on different aspects of a concept, but all think-pair-share groups might be working on the same problem or question. Both approaches can be used effectively in the right setting.

Case Studies

Another effective approach that you can include in your lesson plans is case studies. This reflective technique allows the students to put themselves into a situation or problem and imagine how they would apply the content to that setting. The process is simple: give students all the important details about a real or made-up case involving the subject matter you are discussing, and then supply them with a set of questions that they are to respond to either as a large group or small group (in some cases, you may be able to give a case study to students for individual work). Richards and Bredfeldt (1998) praise this technique by stating, "This strategy is a great way to generate class interaction and opinions. They can be a means by which implications from the study of a Bible passage are developed" (p. 191). The authors go on to explain that these open-ended stories or studies can be used to give students an opportunity to explore how they can apply the truths of Scripture to real-life situations. Case studies can be used in any learning environment to generate a large group or small group discussion about a certain scenario.

Debates

Do you believe there will be a pre-tribulation rapture or post-tribulation rapture? Are you a Calvinist or an Arminianist? Should we cling to our sacred traditions or seek to embrace the secular methods and models? These are great questions, and students should have the room within our classes to discuss them in an open forum. One of the best ways to do this is through a debate. As you look at your *big ideas*, consider which of them might be considered controversial or ones that may generate differing opinions. Give your students an opportunity to consider and research what they believe about a given topic and have a healthy debate in class. Naturally within many Christian churches, there will be many points that are agreed upon. Some students will not want to challenge the side that they agree with, but don't be afraid to challenge them to examine the opposite side of the argument. This will prepare them to defend what they believe. Part of our job as biblical instructors is to prepare students for what they will encounter at their workplaces or in their own communities. Debating against their own view will enable and empower them to defend their beliefs.

When it comes to structuring a debate, begin by assigning individuals to a team and giving that team a particular side of an issue. Decide on a date for the debate, and then let each team work together to do outside research and prepare for the event. During the debate, give each team a strict five minutes to share about their side of the issue. Then allow each team to give a two-minute rebuttal for points that are disagreed upon. Keep repeating this process until you feel both teams have reached the objective.

Marzano, Pickering, and Pollock (2001) offer several pieces of advice for teachers who wish to use cooperative learning strategies in their learning environments. First of all, they state that organizing groups based on ability levels should be done sparingly. It is temping to put all the smart students into one group, but be wary of doing this as the other groups may benefit from the contributions of those students. Secondly, they advise that groups should be kept rather small in size. Assigning roles to groups larger than eight can be difficult. Lastly, cooperative learning should be applied consistently and systematically but not overused or misused. When you incorporate these strategies in your educational ministry context, you will immediately see how useful they can be. It can be tempting to want to continue doing this many times over the course of the unit. However, it can be overused and loose its luster. Additionally, it can be misused if students are not given adequate time to complete the course work or if groups are not well structured. Each student must be given the opportunity to practice the skills being learning independently and process them so that they can become mastered.

Nonlinguistic Representation Strategies

Marzano and his associates also remind us that students store knowledge in two forms: a linguistic form and an imagery form. The linguistic form is all about semantics. It involves statements that can be stored in their long-term memories. A good example of a linguistic strategy involves student fill-in-the-blank notes (or outlines). Students can use these to memorize main points or verses of Scripture that were emphasized in the lesson. On the other hand, the imagery form of stored knowledge is expressed as mental pictures. These mental pictures help students "add on to" or elaborate on the knowledge they are receiving. The more they are able to elaborate on what they are learning, the easier it will be to understand it and recall it. With this in mind, the authors conclude that students will more apt to recall the information they are taught when teachers include both the linguistic form and imagery form in the lesson. Below I will discuss several **nonlinguistic representation strategies** that connect with the imagery form of learning. These strategies will challenge students to generate mental pictures that go along with the information they are learning and then crafting graphic representations of that information. After this, I will explore several linguistic strategies that can help you balance your approach.

Graphic Organizers

Probably the most widely used nonlinguistic representation strategy is graphic organizers. Graphic organizers facilitate the learning process by organizing newly acquired content and/or ideas in picture form. They combine the linguistic and nonlinguistic modes by using words and phrases that are linked by symbols and arrows that represent the relationships between them. Katherine McKnight (2010) recognizes that graphic organizers help students internalize what they are learning as they present the material in both visual and spatial modalities (referring to multiple intelligences). When integrated into the learning environment, she states that graphic organizers "support students by enabling them to literally see connections and relationships between facts, information, and terms" (p. 1). In this way, they have the potential to increase student understanding and retention of material.

Graphic organizers are often compared and/or contrasted with class outlines that are more systematic in nature. Robinson and Kiewra (1995) define an outline as "a systematic listing of a concept with its subordinate concepts and their attribute values" (p. 455). They go on to add that outlines are useful because they include only the most important text information and they convey hierarchical concept relations. Teachers often use this mode of teaching in their lectures because it helps students recognize what is important in a textbook lesson or what should be emphasized during a lecture. Students then are easily able to copy down these outline notes from the teacher and use them to study for an exam. However, as Robinson and Kiewra point out, traditional outlines are not designed to help students discover the relationships among concepts. Graphic organizers, on the other hand, are able to bridge this gap as they present the key ideas and how they relate to each other.

While this book does not lend itself to an explanation of all the different types of graphic organizers that are being used by teachers today, I do want to mention several of the more popular types. The first one is a **power-thinking graphic organizer**. As McKnight (2010) explains, these organizers allow learners to organize ideas and information hierarchically. It can be used to group terms, ideas, and vocabulary words into main headings and subheadings (much like an outline but in visual form). Starting with a main theme or concept at the top of a page (or at the side of the page), teachers can add information at differing power levels. Connect or link concepts with arrows or lines so students can see their relationships (see figure 8).

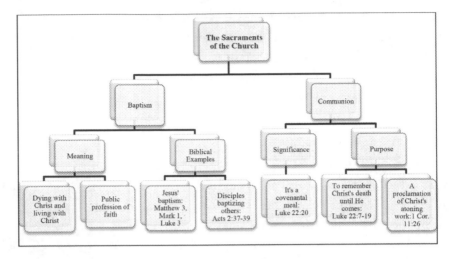

Figure 8: Power-Thinking Graphic Organizer (The Sacraments of the Church)

A second type of graphic organizer is called an **idea web**. Similar to the power-thinking organizer, the idea web explains concepts by branching out into different levels. However, the difference is that instead of being at the top of the page, the main concept or theme is in the middle. As concepts are branched out, it makes the organizer look like a spiderweb. McKnight explains that this organizer "allows learners to organize information in a visual format. Unlike a standard linear outline, the idea web makes the connections among ideas and details more evident" (p. 44). Teachers can use an idea web as a brainstorming activity with students or in a large group discussion. You may even want to consider having students summarize biblical themes from certain passages in an idea web (see examples of this as adapted from class notes taken at Central Bible College in figure 9 and figure 10).

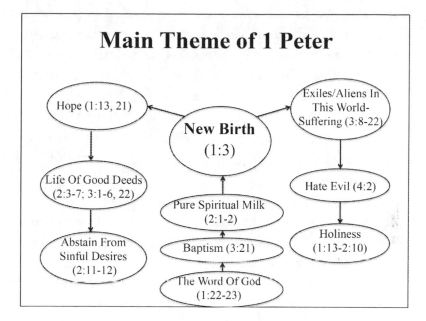

Figure 9: Idea Web (The Main Theme of 1 Peter)

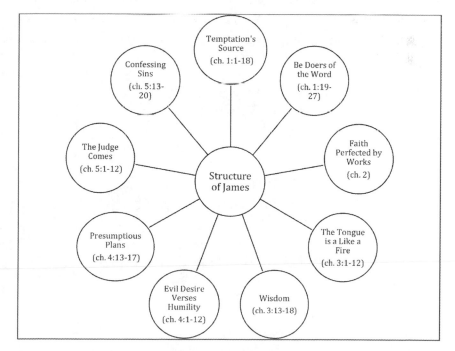

Figure 10: Idea Web (The Structure of James)

The **Venn diagram** is also a popular graphic organizer. In a nutshell, Venn diagrams are composed of two overlapping circles, where each side represents differences and the middle represents the similarities between the two. McKnight further explains that they "provide a visual comparison of similarities and differences between subjects" (p. 12). If you remember, I used a Venn diagram in chapter 5 of this book while describing how to organize lessons thematically. Refer back to that chapter if you want to see an example of this graphic organizer.

A fourth example of a graphic organizer is simply called a *cycle*. It is designed to help students learn about a series of events or reoccurring patterns that occur in a text or a lesson. An easy way to incorporate this method comes from the book of Judges. Following the death of Joshua, the Israelites fell into a pattern where they would first rebel, then God would raise up an enemy against them, then Israel would repent, and lastly, God would save and restore them through one of the judges. This cycle occurs over and over in the book of Judges, but I think the concept can best be understood through visual representation (a cycle graphic organizer). See figure 11 for this demonstration.

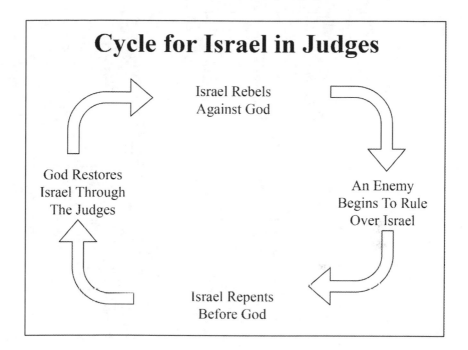

Figure 11: Cycle Graphic Organizer (The Book of Judges)

The last type of graphic organizer that I want to discuss is relatively new, but I believe it has the potential to take our classes to a whole new level in understanding. **Sketch noting** utilizes current technology (such as iPads and iPhones) to take notes with diagrams, charts, and/or drawings (see figure 12 for an example from a friend of mine at church as she was taking notes from a sermon on Acts 15). For more information about the technology behind sketch noting, go to the website: https://www.fiftythree.com. On this site, you will find helpful tools and video tutorials about the process.

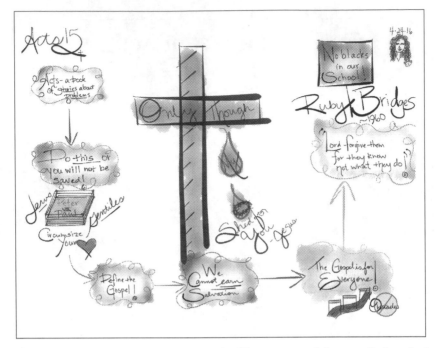

Figure 12: Sketch Noting Example (Courtesy of Anissa Labrador)

Alternative Nonlinguistic Approaches

Nonlinguistic strategies may also be realized through several other means. For example, you may want to consider having students create *physical models* or *draw pictures* that represent what they've learned. Physical models can be created using Play-Doh or even LEGOs. I have used this technique in my classes with great success and have seen other teachers use it as well. It's a great opportunity to involve students in the learning process, especially when they are able to present their project and expound on how it fits into the bigger picture. You can also use different forms of *media* to emphasize points in your learning environment. Maybe add a video clip to a lesson or sermon to help illustrate your point. A fitting song can also underscore what you are trying to communicate. Lastly, as Marzano, Pickering, and Pollock (2001) suggest, let students engage in *kinesthetic activity*. These are activities that involve physical movement. The authors note, "Physical movement associated with specific knowledge generates a mental image of the knowledge in the mind of the learner" (p. 82). They go on to state that kinesthetic learning activities can often be a natural and enjoyable way to express knowledge.

Traditional Linguistic Strategies

As important as nonlinguistic strategies are, I believe we should also incorporate traditional linguistic strategies in our lesson plans to stay balanced in our approach. These strategies are best utilized in conjunction with lectures. For instance, you can use a "drill and practice" strategy that will involve the repetition of skills or facts as learned in class (especially for the purpose of memorization). Math teachers often use this teaching method because students need to be drilled with math problems that will help them understand concepts. Similarly, you may want to drill your students with Bible verses or practical biblical study skills. This is also where you can have them practice with mnemonic devices. Rod Evans (2007) explains that **mnemonic devices** are techniques or strategies for improving or strengthening memory. The idea behind mnemonic devices is to help students learn to recall concepts by thinking of a memorable sentence. The first letter of each word in the sentence, when put together, forms the mnemonic. There are two popular forms of mnemonics that are widely used today: acrostics and acronyms. According to Evans, acrostic mnemonics are sentences in which with the first letter of each word is a letter of one of the concepts that needs to be remembered. Acrostics are most helpful for long lists of concepts that must be memorized. For example, music teachers often give their students the acrostic "EGBDF" (every good boy deserves fudge) to help them learn the notes on a music staff. On the other hand, as Evans goes on to explain, acronyms utilize the first letter of each word to spell out a word or phrase. Scientists often refer to the color spectrum as the acronym "ROY G. BIV" (red, orange, yellow, green, blue, indigo, violet). Another example Evans gives includes the word "SCUBA" (self-contained underwater breathing apparatus).

Employing mnemonic devices in lessons can be a fun and meaningful way to teach.

Another linguistic strategy involves *provocative questions and discussions*. Richards and Bredfeldt (1998) propose that provocative questions encourage student learning, and they are, in fact, an essential part of a teaching strategy. As teachers, we should all want our questions to lead to meaningful discussions with students. That was definitely the case in Jesus's ministry as he was often asked questions or offered them to others as a way to spark conversation with people. These inquiries always led to further dialogue. For today's learning environments, Richards and Bredfeldt suggest that teachers plan ahead and create good questions before their lesson. Unfortunately, many teachers today try to come up with good questions on the fly, but that is hard to do and often less effective. You may want to consider creating questions that are aligned to Bloom's Taxonomy (as discussed in chapter 4). As you may recall, Bloom's Revised Taxonomy states that students should be able to remember, understand, apply, analyze, evaluate, and create. These potential outcomes should challenge us to consider what kind of thinking will promote deeper understand and skill development so they can build on what they already know. As stated earlier, don't settle for simple or lower levels of learning; aim for deeper level transfer. This also means teachers should turn aside from "closed" questions that only look for a single word answer and don't allow for further discussion. Instead, as Richards and Bredfeldt suggest, generate open-ended questions that will fuel student involvement and help the group see and make application for their lives. A closed question would ask, "How many of the disciples became martyrs for their faith?" On the other hand, an open-ended question would seek to trigger a discussion by asking, "If you were alive in the New Testament era, what would you do and how would you feel if you were being hunted and people wanted to execute you for your faith?" Larry Lindquist (2010) adds to this dialogue by recommending that teachers make their questions accessible to everyone by making sure students understand the terms in each question. Additionally, teachers should refrain from asking more than one question at a time or trying to put words in the mouths of students by stating something like, "Don't you think that—" or "In what ways are you like the Pharisees in this passage?" Instead, let them grapple with the implications of the question at hand. As you dialogue with your class, try to get everyone involved and hear his or her thoughts on the subjects you are teaching.

Lastly, any opportunity you have to get students to reflect on what they are learning will be a beneficial experience. **Reflective journaling** is a great way to do this as it allows students to reflect or contemplate on the thoughts or feelings they have toward a text or a concept they are learning during a lecture (Coley, Hantla, and Cobb, 2013). McKnight and Berlage (2007) add that students' personal thoughts or responses help them to develop a personal connection with the material and their own writing. You can encourage your students to use reflective journals in class, or you may choose to assign them as homework (maybe even as your summative assessment). Either way, be sure to include questions that cannot be answered in one or two sentences. Instead, make them write out at least a paragraph, which will give them the space to really wrestle with the implications of each question.

Choosing the Best Strategy for Your Educational Ministry

In his book, *Multiple Intelligences in the Classroom*, Thomas Armstrong (2000) proposes that teachers choose their instructional strategies based on each of the eight multiple intelligences that are expressed in the learning environment. If you remember from chapter 2 of this book, Howard Gardner proposed that there are eight intellectual competences that lead to greater learning in each student (he later added a possible ninth to the list): linguistic intelligence, logical-mathematical intelligence, musical intelligence, spatial intelligence, bodily-kinesthetic intelligence, interpersonal intelligence, intrapersonal intelligence, and natural intelligence. Learners in your educational ministry context who are more interpersonal in nature may naturally gravitate toward strategies that incorporate cooperative groups. According to Armstrong, these are your learners who love to bounce ideas off other people. On the other hand, intrapersonal individuals (those who are more in touch with their own feelings and motivations) may prefer activities they can do by themselves, like reflective journaling or drill and practice (linguistic strategies). They need time alone and the opportunity to have self-paced projects so they can share their feelings, plan, and set goals. Nonlinguistic representation strategies will be more suited for learners who are either visual/spatial, musical, or kinesthetic. Visual or spatial intelligence individuals like to create mental images or pictures to solve problems. They need graphics, art, movie illustrations, slides, and puzzles. Similarly, kinesthetic learners will be drawn to nonlinguistic strategies because they have opportunity to incorporate hands-on experiences. I also lump musical intelligence personalities into this category because they learn from songs that you can use as illustrations or they may have the talent to create songs that help them better learn the material. Lastly, traditional linguistic strategies are useful to reach verbal/linguistic and logical-mathematical students. Verbal/linguistic learners enjoy manipulating words to express them creatively or poetically. They love to read, write, and tell stories, and that is why they enjoy engaging with a teacher's questions and discussions. Logical-mathematical students learn by reasoning and experimenting. They want to see patterns, reason deductively, and think logically. That is why they may enjoy the drill and practice strategy.

Another approach to planning teaching strategies was illustrated by Richards and Bredfeldt (1998), who suggested that teachers filter each potential teaching strategy through a four-question grid or filter: Who are my learners? What is the lesson aim? What part of the lesson? What resources will I need? First of all, consider who your learners are and the unique characteristics they bring to the table (refer back to chapter 2 for a refresher about building learner profiles). Based on the demographics of your class, you will want to make sure that your teaching methods, for instance, are culturally relevant and appropriate for the age group you are teaching. The activities that youth groups enjoy may not go over well with adult groups. When it comes to the second question referring to a lesson's aims (i.e., goals or objectives), refrain from choosing an activity or teaching method just because it is fun. Make sure it relates to the lesson's goals and furthers student understanding. The third question challenges teachers to take into consideration the organizational structure that has been selected (as discussed earlier in this chapter). Some teaching methods may only be appropriate for the body of the lesson, while others can be saved for an introduction or conclusion. The last question refers to the resources and/or class materials that are an important consideration in this process. Consider what kinds of resources you will need for your teaching strategy. Will you include a PowerPoint presentation or class handouts? Will you need to find a video on youtube.com or a video clip that fits your lesson and illustrates your points? What about incorporating a musical selection or an article that emphasizes your big ideas? These kinds of resources can affect the teaching strategies you select.

Furthermore, Richards and Bredfeldt suggest that teachers tie their delivery strategies to their lesson or unit goal's learning domains (at the macro level as discussed in chapter 4). If you remember, the cognitive domain involves one's thinking abilities (knowing facts, terms, and details). If your educational goal involves this domain, then consider adding brainstorming activities, case studies, debates, interviews, or panel discussions to your lectures. Secondly, the affective domain seeks to impact a student's values and attitudes. Educational goals in this domain may be achieved when teachers model the truth for them. Richards and Bredfeldt point out that Jesus often modeled his teaching through his own actions. Consider for example how he washed his disciple's feet when trying to teach them what it means to be a servant. He demonstrated for them what that means. To this end, consider strategies that will impact the heart: dramas, testimonies, video illustrations, as well as taking them on mission trips, community service projects, nursing homes, prisons. The authors comment, "Any method that goes beyond simply filling the head to affecting the heart is appropriately categorized an affective methodology" (p. 185). Lastly, the behavioral domain is meant to motivate action based on the material that is presented. Do you want them to change a behavior or develop a new skill? The best way to incorporate these domains is to demonstrate the behavior you wish to be emulated and reinforce that behavior. For this, you may want to include workshops, experiments, role-plays, or practice sessions.

Conclusion

We shouldn't teach just to teach. That's a dangerous way to approach education! Instead, we should teach for learning and understanding. Likewise, we shouldn't diversify our teaching methods simply for the sake of diversifying. We differentiate, first of all, because everyone is different and that means everyone learns differently. Along with this, we recognize that learning increases exponentially when students are engaged with the lesson. That is why we should make every effort possible to expand our "teaching toolbox" in pursuit of transferring knowledge to our students. That is what Jesus did and what we should emulate.

This consideration should lead to the development of both an organizational strategy and a delivery strategy. An organizational strategy involves your lesson's framework or structure, which determines the sequence of learning. There are numerous opinions on what this structure should look like, but the important thing is to make sure that it is a reflection of the target audience. In other words, think about what structure will help the students in your educational ministry the best. This may change from time to time. On the flip side, your delivery strategy will include the actual teaching methods you will employ. Again, the methods you choose should reflect the needs of those in your sphere of influence. Hopefully, you will be able to utilize some active learning techniques that will help students engage the material you are teaching. This process is all about being creative and pursuing excellence!

Practice Makes Perfect

Graphic Organizers Worksheet

Directions: Now is your chance to create some graphic organizers. You can copy these graphic organizers or create your own using Microsoft Word on your computer.

Power-Thinking Graphic Organizer

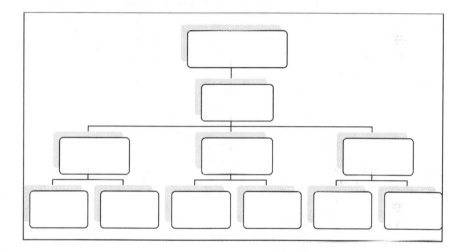

Venn Diagram

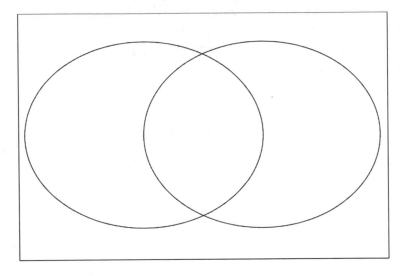

Idea Web

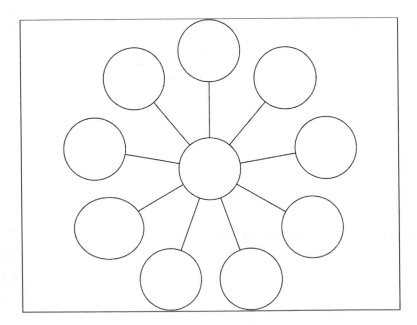

Sources

Armstrong, T. *Multiple Intelligences in the Classroom*. Alexandria, Virginia: ASCD, 2000.

Bain, K. *What the Best College Teachers Do*. Cambridge, Massachusetts: Harvard University Press, 2004.

Coley, K. S. "Active learning techniques in the Christian education classroom and in ministry contexts." *Christian Education Journal*, 9 (2012): 357–371.

Coley, K., B. Hantla, and C. Cobb. *Best Practices for Beginning a Flipped Classroom in the Humanities*. Paper presented at the NAPCE Annual Conference in Chicago, Illinois, October 2013.

Dick, W. O., L. Carey, and J. O. Carey. *The Systematic Design of Instruction*. 7th ed. Englewood Cliffs, New Jersey: Merrill, 2011.

Evans, R. *Every Good Boy Deserves Fudge: The Book of Mnemonic Devices*. New York, New York: Penguin Books, 2007.

Eyre, E. (n.d.). *Gagne's Nine Levels of Learning: Training Your Team Effectively*.

Retrieved from http://www.mindtools.com/pages/article/gagne.htm.

Ferdinando, K. "Jesus, the Theological Educator." *Themelios*, 38 (2013): 360–74.

Gagne's Nine Events of Instruction. University of Florida's Center for Technology and Training. (2015). Retrieved from http://citt.ufl.edu/tools/gagnes-9-events-of-instruction/.

Gardner, H. *Frames of Mind: The Theory of Multiple Intelligences.* New York, New York: Basic Books, 1983.

Hendricks, H. *Teaching to Change Lives.* Colorado Springs, Colorado: Multnomah Books, 1987.

LeFever, M. D. *Learning Styles: Reaching Everyone God Gave You to Teach.* Colorado Springs, Colorado: David C. Cook, 2004.

Lindquist, L. (2010). "Asking Questions." Class presentation, Foundations of Teaching and Learning, Denver Seminary, Littleton, Colorado, 2010.

Marzano, R. J., D. J. Pickering, and J. E. Pollock. *Classroom Instruction That Works: Research-Based Strategies for Increasing Student Achievement.* Alexandria, Virginia: ASCD, 2001.

McCarthy, B, and D. McCarthy. *Teaching around the 4MAT® Cycle: Designing Instruction for Diverse Learners with Diverse Learning Styles.* Thousand Oaks, California: Corwin Press, 2006.

McKnight, K. S., and B. P. Berlage. *Teaching the Classics in the Inclusive Classroom: Reader Response Activities to Engage All Learners.* San Fransisco, California: Jossey-Bass Teacher, 2007.

McKnight, K. S. *The Teacher's Big Book of Graphic Organizers: 100 Reproducible Organizers that Help Kids with Reading, Writing, and the Content Areas.* San Francisco, California: Jossey-Bass, 2010.

Richards, L. O., and G. O. Bredfeldt. *Creative Bible Teaching.* Chicago, Illinois: Moody Bible Institute, 1998.

Robinson, D. H., and K. A. Kiewra. "Visual Argument: Graphic Organizers Are Superior to Outlines in Improving Learning from Text." *Journal of Educational Psychology*, 87 (1995): 455-467.

Schunk, D. *Learning Theories: An Educational Perspective.* Boston, Massachusetts: Pearson, 2012.

Schimmels, C. *Teaching That Works: Strategies from Scripture for Classrooms Today.* Cincinnati, Ohio: Howe Design, 1999.

Smith, P. L., and T. J. Ragan. *Instructional Design.* 3rd ed. Upper Saddle River, New Jersey: Wiley & Sons, Inc., 2005.

8

DESIGN ASSESSMENTS AND PROVIDE FEEDBACK

Let us imagine an educative assessment
system that is designed to improve,
not just audit, student performance.

—Grant Wiggins

Preach the word; be prepared in season and out of season;
correct, rebuke and encourage—with great
patience and careful instruction.

—2 Timothy 4:2 (NIV)

For a number of years early in my teaching career, I had the opportunity to be a guitar instructor for my school. Most of the students I taught were beginners, which meant it was the first time they were exposed to how to read music and chord charts. As one might expect, there was much difficultly in the beginning for each student. They would often play wrong notes, forget the rhythm, and/ or complain because of the new calluses that had formed on the tips of their fingers. Despite these challenges, I was always impressed with their resolve, as they genuinely wanted to learn how to play the guitar. They had a goal in mind, and they stuck to it.

The greatest lesson I learned through this process was the importance of assessment and feedback. I gleaned more about these two concepts from teaching an instrument than I ever did in a classroom setting. I quickly discovered that students learning to play an instrument require constant assessment and feedback from their instructor. It only takes one wrong note to make a whole chord sound sour. This may be due to a student not pressing their finger down hard enough on the neck of the guitar or having their finger in the wrong place. Effective instructors will not only point out these mistakes but also help students correct them. They will also model how to play it the right way so students can see it and/or hear it for themselves.

Are we, as Christian educators, dedicating as much time and energy to assessments and feedback as music teachers do on a regular basis? I think we can and we should! In every educational ministry context, there is a need for quality assessment practices. Students need to be given attentive assessments and feedback in order to achieve the educational goals that we have created. That is why some would argue that a class is only as strong as its assessments. A teacher cannot know if a student has really learned anything without some sort of assessment. As one of my professors used to always say, "Teaching without assessing is only talking."

Assessments are necessary because teachers need to know the answers to two questions: what is going on, and why is it going on? If students do not understand your material because of something you are doing (or not doing), then you need to change your instruction. On the other hand, if your students are failing to understand the material because they are not paying attention, then they need to make their own adjustments. In sum, assessments give the answer to whether the problem is you as the teacher or them as the students. Will you change your instruction or seek to change your student's learning behavior? The key in all this is in learning how to better observe your students and ask them good questions so you can determine how lessons can be adjusted in a way that will increase learning. This is not about a grade but instead an opportunity to encourage learning.

As mentioned earlier in this book, the apostle Paul made it a point to assess the needs of early Christians before advancing them to the "meat" of God's Word. The author of Hebrews addresses a similar concern in Hebrews 5:11–12a (NIV) when he states: "We have much to say about this, but it is hard to make it clear to you because you no longer try to understand. In fact, though by this time you ought to be teachers, you need someone to teach you the elementary truths of God's word all over again." What I find most interesting about this passage is the fact that these early Christians were no longer trying to understand. They had been given the information they needed (in this context, knowledge about the supremacy of Christ), but it was not sinking in. Because of this, they needed to hear it again and again until it clicked. The author assessed that the problem was not with the content delivered, nor the speaker, but with the audience. Knowing the difference is a skill that all Christian educators need to grow in before plowing ahead with new information; their students may not be ready for it.

That is why the focus of this chapter is on designing effective assessments (both formative and summative) for your specific educational ministry. Assessments come in all shapes and sizes, but the most important thing is to create assessments that will be geared for your specific audience. Additionally, this chapter will give you into several tips for giving effective feedback to your students. Without feedback, students will be unsure of the areas where they need to grow (spiritually and intellectually). Unfortunately, many Christian educators skip over these essential aspects of education, but I believe it's time to refocus our time and energy on learning how to better evaluate those we teach.

Designing Formative and Summative Assessments

Back in chapter 4, I described the process of creating educational goals, and I challenged you to come up with a summative assessment for how you will evaluate whether or not students achieved the educational goal. I also mentioned that there are two types of assessments: formative and summative. **Formative assessments** are conducted during a term of learning to help the teacher determine where students are at in their understanding of certain concepts. **Summative assessments**, on the other hand, include the evaluations of students at the end of the course or class to gauge whether or not all the goals and objectives have been met. In this section, I will introduce you to several formative and summative assessment strategies that you can incorporate into your educational ministry, and I will explain how you can implement them in your specific context. The more tools (alternative assessments) you have in your teaching toolbox, the more effective you will be.

Formative Assessments

An easy way to understand formative assessments is to refer to them as "checks along the way." This concept is similar to what many middle and high school textbooks do as they break up chapters into sections. At the end of every segment is a section checkup, review, or quiz. The purpose of these is to make sure that as students are progressing through a chapter, they are not missing out on important concepts. Students are required to go back through the section, answer questions, and highlight important people, places, and terms to know. Similarly, as you progress through a Bible lesson or a series of lessons, you will want to ensure that students are not only paying attention but also understanding each segment of the material.

Consider how you can perform quick checks to assess their comprehension. This can be done simply through having them give a thumbs-up or thumbs-down based on how well they feel they understand the content. If someone gives a thumbs-down, then go back and review the parts of the material that were missed or misunderstood. You can also ask your students at the end of class to give a metaphor for how they are feeling about the content. "As you leave today, do you feel like a zombie, a runner, or an elephant (who never forgets), and why do you feel this way?" The stoplight is another popular formative assessment. For this, ask students to give you a green light to keep going with the material because they understand it very well, a yellow light if they are kind of getting it but not quite there, or a red light if they are not getting it at all. Asking questions and giving verbal quizzes about the content can also be a valuable assessment tool for you. In this strategy, teachers call on students to answer questions about the content verbally, or have them write answers down on pieces of paper and turn them in at the end of class. Similarly, you can collect your students' class notes to evaluate how well they are paying attention and grasping the material. I did this several years ago after preaching a sermon on the importance of worship. Before my sermon, I handed out note cards to everyone and gave them five minutes to answer questions about the sermon when I had finished. Not everyone turned in their cards, but I found this to be very informative for the ones who did. As I mentioned in the last chapter, you can also have students create their own graphic organizer or break them up into smaller groups where they can discuss questions about the topic being presented. The options for formative assessments are endless, but the important thing is to find whatever it is that works for you in your educational ministry context so you can make sure everyone is on the same page and you can urge everyone to keep moving forward.

Summative Assessments

By the end of your course, you will want to ensure that each student is able to demonstrate his or her mastery of the material. This is accomplished through a final summative assessment. The type of summative assessment you design should be determined by the classification of your educational goals at the macro level (refer back to chapter 4 to review macro and micro educational goals). Your goals at this classification level will be cognitive, affective, or behavioral. For cognitive educational goals, you may want to consider creating an objective-style test (also known as a selected response assessment). According to Stiggins (1997), these assessments are designed to draw out certain answers from students that will inform teachers of whether or not students have absorbed the subject matter. Tests can also assess students' reasoning abilities, when questions require students to use their knowledge to solve problems or figure something out.

Objective-style tests or exams are usually composed of true/false, short answer, matching, multiple-choice, and/or completion questions. However, I also want to urge you to include essay questions in your exams or give students separate essay assignments. Stiggins proposes that essays may have the greatest untapped potential of any of the other types of questions. Essays allow teachers to "tap at least some of our most highly valued, complex, achievement targets at a fraction of the cost of performance assessments. Essays can delve into student attainment of some complex and sophisticated achievement targets. They can assess these outcomes with low time and energy for teacher" (p. 151). Students usually spend more time studying for essays than other possible questions because they have to analyze and reflect deeply on the material covered in class. That is why it's advisable to make them worth more points than the other questions on your exams.

You may also want to consider giving students a pretest and a posttest. A pretest assesses students at the beginning of a course or unit, while a posttest examines how much they have learned by the end of it. For example, if you want to measure your students' level of biblical literacy, then give them a test at the beginning of your course and then at the end. This technique will help you measure how much they have progressed in their knowledge of the Bible, and it will inform you of areas where they still need assistance.

When designing test questions, be sure to align them with the exact behavior described in your educational goals or instructional objectives. For instance, if one of your educational goals stated, "Students will be able to discuss the three main themes of the book of John—signs, belief, and life (as discerned from John 20:30–31)," then you would want to make sure there are questions on the test that assesses whether or not they have achieved this goal. You may want them write an essay that requires them to explain these themes and show concrete examples from the book of John where the themes are evident.

Let me give you another example that will include other types of questions. Suppose your educational goal stated, "Students will be able to identify the major events (and their corresponding dates) that help us see the process whereby the biblical canon was formed." In this case, you may want to create a matching section on your test that would require students to pair up major events with their corresponding dates (see figure 13 for a depiction of this).

Section 1: Match these dates with the corresponding event:
A. 621 B.C.
B. 421 B.C.
C. 250 B.C.
D. 397 A.D.
E. 90 A.D.
1. _____ Council of Jamnia (OT Scriptures sealed)
2. _____ Nehemiah 8 (Ezra reads the law after the exile)
3. _____ Greek translation of the Bible (The Septuagint was written)
4. _____ Council of Carthage (NT Scriptures sealed)
5. _____ 2 Kings 22-23 (Workman finds the Book of the Law and reads it to King Josiah)

Figure 13: Depiction of Test Items That Are Aligned to Educational Goals

In table 6, you will see a list of frequent verbs that are used in educational goals and instructional objectives accompanied by the type of test question that may be employed to assess a student's comprehension of the material (adapted from Dick, Carey, and Carey, 2011).

Educational Goal/Objective Verbs:	Options for Test Questions					
	Completion	Short Answer	Matching	Multiple Choice	True/False	Essay
State/Name	X	X				
Define	X	X	X	X		
Identify	X	X	X	X	X	
Discriminate		X	X	X	X	
Select		X	X	X	X	
Locate		X	X	X		
Evaluate/Judge		X	X	X	X	X
Solve		X	X	X		X
Discuss						X
Develop						X
Construct						X
Generate						X
Choose			X	X	X	X

Table 6: Aligning Educational Goals with Test Questions

Additional options for assessing cognitive goals may include having students recite memory verses or requiring them to hand in their notes at the end of the unit or course. You may even want to have them create a graphic organizer that represents the main ideas you expressed in class. These are great ways to gauge student comprehension of the material.

Affective educational goals are more difficult to assess but nonetheless important. These goals are concerned with the learner's attitudes or preferences. To measure educational goals in this domain, consider asking students to self-report (or self-monitor) their progress in the areas you are focusing on. Ask them questions such as these: "Are the fruits of the Spirit being displayed through your life more this year than last year? Do you pray have personal devotions and on a regular basis? How well do you show your love to your spouse? How quick are you to give in to your sinful desires when no one else is looking?" Questions like these that measure a person's heart response can be given through a Likert scale (questions that ask if students strongly agree, agree, are neutral, disagree, or strongly disagree). Self-reporting helps them become responsible for their own growth and learning. As Lorna Earl (2003) states, "If they are to become critical thinkers and problem solvers who can bring their talents and their knowledge to bear on their decisions and actions, they have to develop skills of self-assessment and self-adjustment. They can't just wait for someone to tell them the right answer" (p. 101). Hopefully, your goal as a teacher is to help students become lifelong learners that will consistently apply the concepts of the Bible to their lives. For this to happen, you need to challenge them to assess their attitudes on a regular basis: "How have I grown in this area? Where am I still lacking? What can I do to improve?" They can't figure out the answers to these questions by reading a book; they have to look inward. With affective goals, you are looking to assess their heart response.

Affective goals may also be assessed through personal journals or reflection papers that require them to grapple with the material in a personal manner. These assessments will help you understand their emotions and their decision-making processes. Additionally, consider ways in which you can observe their attitudes outside the learning environment. If your educational goal involves service, then observe them on a trip to feed the homeless, or on a visit to the widows and orphans in your area, etc. Watch for their attitudes when they do seemingly menial projects like stacking chairs after service or coming early to church to start the coffee machine. Our students need to know that attitudes matter, and the more we can do as teachers to assess our student's attitudes, the better we will be able to help them grow in Christlikeness.

Lastly, behavioral educational goals can be evaluated by observing how well a learner performs a sequence of steps. Teachers must make sure that students have mastered certain skills or are able to meet certain standards. Consider giving students a portfolio assignment at the end of your unit of instruction that will assess their ability in certain areas. Portfolios will include a collection of work samples that students have been working on throughout the unit. Evaluate how well the portfolios are organized, how clear they are, and whether or not there is congruence between the information and skills learned and how they are performed. Another way to assess this domain is through live performances. This is a popular method for music teachers. Their summative assessment will undoubtedly include a musical recital. Similarly, if you are teaching students how to evangelize, then take them out on an excursion like a mission trip and observe their interaction with people. If you are teaching a class on prayer, have them write out a prayer (given certain parameters of your choosing) and recite it in front of the group.

Once you have established what your summative assessment will entail, you will need to develop a response format that will show whether or not students lived up to your expectations (Dick, Carey, and Carey, 2011). What level of performance must be shown in order for you to consider that learners have mastered this unit? Will you use a checklist (yes, they passed; or no, they didn't)? Will you use a rating scale that requires certain levels of quality (poor, adequate, or good)? Will you use a frequency count (occurrences of each required element when observed)? In order to help students understand what will be expected of them, Earl (2003) suggests that teachers give students visual examples of what "good work looks like" when a project is completed. This is important because teachers often expect their students to automatically know what is expected, but students do not always live up to expectations because they do not have good examples of what "excellence" looks like. Effective teachers will always tell students exactly what is expected. In other words, students need to be able to see where they are aiming. This is why it would be beneficial to incorporate rubrics in your educational ministry (I will describe these more in detail in the next section).

Giving Feedback to Students

Teachers routinely use the information from assessments to help them plan for future lessons, but this information can also be given to students, in the form of feedback, to improve their learning as teachers help bring clarity to areas that require improvement. Earl (2003) defines **feedback** as information that gives students direct and usable insights into their current performance. This means students can use feedback to adjust their understanding about a subject or to rethink their ideas. It can also lead to increased effort or engagement in students. The key is for teachers to give the kind of feedback that encourages student learning and gives students signposts or directions that will guide them in the process. Below are some guidelines that may help you in your pursuit of giving effective feedback to students.

Feedback should be given in a timely manner.

When you were in college, did you ever take a test or write a research paper only to have waited for weeks until the professor graded it and got it back to you? How helpful was that feedback weeks after it was turned in? More than likely, it was not very helpful. You probably moved on to another subject or had to write another paper before knowing what your professor was even looking for. This can be very frustrating for students, and it can cause them to lose their motivation to learn and work hard. That is why Marzano, Pickering, and Pollock (2001) suggest that feedback should be given in a timely fashion, whatever the context. Immediate feedback is always the best because a longer delay will result in less improvement when it comes to student accomplishment.

Feedback should be more descriptive than evaluative.

According to Earl (2003), feedback does not need to be formal, but it should be more descriptive than evaluative. Evaluative feedback involves giving short comments to students after an assignment or assessment. The comments are not usually specific. In more formal classes, evaluative feedback is actually necessary, usually for a grade. For example, the teacher must decide if the student was able to study a given passage and identify the big idea or decipher whether or not a student correctly used a particular biblical interpretation method that was described in class. Students either did or didn't do these things. In these cases, the teacher will grade the student and simply tell him or her if the requirement was met or not. Earl informs us that this type of feedback may tell a student whether he or she is doing okay in a class, but it fails to give students direction for how the learning process should move forward. That is why there is also a need for descriptive feedback.

Descriptive feedback, according to Earl, addresses the wrong ways students interpreted a question or assignment, and it clears up any misunderstanding. It is intentional about helping students grapple with areas where they struggled, not just succeeded. In this way, it becomes "corrective" in nature, which means it provides students with an explanation for what they are doing that is correct or incorrect. Simply telling a student that he or she got an answer wrong on an exam will not have as positive of an impact as it would if it were accompanied by the right answer and an explanation as to why it is wrong (Marzano, Pickering, and Pollock, 2001). Descriptive feedback also prevents us as teachers from using useless phrases that offer little value or make students feel that their work was only good or bad (e.g., awesome, great, wonderful, brilliant, boring). These terms do not help people moving forward in their education (Kurtz, Silverman, and Draper, 1998). In fact, Earl (2003) states that feedback that is vague or faulty may lead to students making inappropriate modifications to their work or they might not notice that they need to make adjustments at all. Lastly, descriptive feedback should also give students the "next step" they need based on an image of what "good work looks like." In other words, students will know what the finished product should look like when they arrive at the educational goal. This will help students begin to take on more responsibility in the learning process as they learn to self-assess and self-correct. In sum, evaluative feedback gives only rewards and punishments or approval/disapproval, but descriptive feedback describes to students why an answer is correct and explains what is being achieved or not achieved. It helps students look for better ways of doing something or suggesting ways they can improve themselves (Earl, 2003).

Feedback should reinforce effort and provide recognition (reward effort).

Marzano, Pickering, and Pollock (2001) challenge teachers to address their students' attitudes and beliefs about the educational process. The authors argue that if students believe they have the ability, they can tackle anything. However, not all students realize the importance of effort. That is why teachers need to be intentional about explaining and exemplifying an "effort belief" to their students. This involves teaching them about the connection between effort and achievement.

When I taught middle school math, I had a student who was concerned because she received a *B* as her final first semester grade (it was her only *B* of the semester). She came to me asking what she needed to do to get an *A* in the subsequent semester. I challenged her to keep working hard and do more practice problems, and if she had questions, she could come to me and I would help tutor her before school started in the mornings. Her attitude and response was something I will never forget. Her effort that next semester was off the charts. She was so determined to get an *A* that she spent countless hours going over and over each math concept with me and her parents at home. I kid you not; she only missed a handful of questions the entire semester (homework, quizzes, and tests included). I have never been more impressed with any single student in my whole career in teaching. What made the greatest difference for her? It was her parents and I reinforcing her effort.

One way teachers can help students keep track of their effort is by creating an effort and achievement rubric. For example, when it comes to their effort, Marzano and his coauthors suggest asking students to answer questions on a scale of one to four (4 = excellent; 3 = good; 2 = needs improvement; 1 = unacceptable).

- I worked on the task until it was completed.
- I pushed myself to continue working on the task even when difficulties arose.
- I viewed difficulties that arose as opportunities to strengthen my understanding.
- I put some effort into the task, but I stopped working when difficulties arose.
- I put very little effort into the task.

Concurrently, you can ask them about their achievements on the same scale (4 = excellent; 3 = good; 2 = needs improvement; 1 = unacceptable).

- I exceeded the objectives of the task or lesson.
- I met the objectives of the task or lesson.
- I met a few of the objectives of the task or lesson but did not meet others.
- I did not meet the objectives of the task or lesson.

The authors also suggest giving recognition to students who go the extra mile. They go on to explain, "Reinforcing effort can help teach students one of the most valuable lessons they can learn—the harder you try, the more successful you are. Providing recognition for attainment of goals enhances achievement and stimulates motivation" (p. 59). So find ways to reward students or offer praise to them when they achieve their goals.

Feedback should be sensitive to abilities that are difficult to change.

As a Christian school teacher, I have often encountered students who speak English as a second language. Assessing these students can be difficult, as they have to translate their thoughts or words into English. I have always tried to extend grace in these situations and work with each student appropriately. Likewise, you may also encounter students who have similar difficulties, or maybe students who display nervous habits (such as constantly saying, "um"), or students who use certain other idioms that are difficult to follow. All these need to be handled gracefully. I would encourage you to be sensitive and be careful in how you evaluate or give feedback in these situations. You can identify certain issues, but be careful to do it in a way that will constructively lead to furthering their education. Furthermore, as Kurtz, Silverman, and Draper (1998) point out, teachers should be sure to focus their feedback on student behavior rather than their personalities. This is important because a student may come across as highly emotional, but simply stating

"You are too emotional" won't help the situation. Instead, consider stating something like this: "When you wrote your story, it came across as overdramatic. Be sure to watch out for this next time, while still including the important elements of the story." Do you see the difference? Take the judgment out and add a little encouragement.

Feedback should involve more than just advice.

In Exodus 18, Moses had just rescued the people of Israel from Egypt, and they were in the midst of traveling toward the Promised Land. During this time, Moses had taken it upon himself to be the judge over all Israel and hear the cases that had come before him from the camp. Unfortunately, this led to the exhaustion of Moses because he was acting alone in this feat, and—when his father-in-law, Jethro, came to see him—it was very evident. Listen to how this story unfolds in verses 14–23.

> When his father-in-law saw all that Moses was doing for the people, he said, "What is this you are doing for the people? Why do you alone sit as judge, while all these people stand around you from morning till evening?" Moses answered him, "Because the people come to me to seek God's will. Whenever they have a dispute, it is brought to me, and I decide between the parties and inform them of God's decrees and instructions." Moses' father-in-law replied, "What you are doing is not good. You and these people who come to you will only wear yourselves out. The work is too heavy for you; you cannot handle it alone. Listen now to me and I will give you some advice, and may God be with you. You must be the people's representative before God and bring their disputes to him. Teach them his decrees and instructions, and show them the way they are to live and how they are to behave. But select capable men from all the people—men

who fear God, trustworthy men who hate dishonest gain—and appoint them as officials over thousands, hundreds, fifties and tens. Have them serve as judges for the people at all times, but have them bring every difficult case to you; the simple cases they can decide themselves. That will make your load lighter, because they will share it with you. If you do this and God so commands, you will be able to stand the strain, and all these people will go home satisfied" (Exodus 18:14–23, NIV).

What is it that Jethro was doing for Moses after assessing the problem? Did he give Moses helpful feedback or simply offer good advice? I believe the later is true. This was not wrong of Jethro (as giving good advice is always a good thing), but for the sake of comparison, I want to point out the differences between advice and feedback. Advice is telling someone what you think he or she should or should not do. It is saying, "You did not give me enough background of the life of Jeremiah. Next time, include five more Scripture references to make sure you have covered your bases." Feedback, on the other hand, encourages students along the way by suggesting several things that can be done to improve. It would involve stating, "It appears that you may have needed more background to complete your character study. I would like to encourage you to next time provide this information through pictures, Scripture references, additional sentences, or even stories."

Feedback should be a natural extension of a rubric.

One year when I was teaching middle school history, I required my students to interview their grandparents to get information about what life was like when they were growing up. Students were to write a one-page report of the interview and hand it in to me along with pictures that portrayed different aspects of their grandparents' lives. I read through each account and gave students grades based on how well I thought they did. Everyone in the class did very well and received either an *A* or an *A-*. I didn't think much of the significance of the grades at the time, because in my mind, they were all so high. But the next day, I received a visit from the principal who told me that she had received some complaints from parents because their student got an *A-* on the project and they thought their child deserved a 100%. I explained that I didn't believe anyone's work deserved that high of a grade as everyone had room for improvement (especially as it was the beginning of the year, as it was their first writing assignment). Nevertheless, the principal encouraged me to develop a **rubric** for the next essay so the students (and their parents) would know exactly what they could improve on.

For those of you unfamiliar with rubrics, they are simply scoring tools that communicate expectations for an assignment to students. Heidi Audrade (2014) explains that rubrics are important because they list the criteria for an assignment or "what counts." They also articulate gradations of quality for each criterion, from excellent to poor. This informs students of how well they must do in order to be considered proficient. As I have grown to understand and utilize rubrics, I have noticed they have not only helped me as a teacher in the grading process, but they have also helped my students as they communicate exactly what I expect from them. Now I strive to give them out to them at the beginning of the class or when a project is first assigned.

There are two variations of grading rubrics that you can incorporate into your educational ministry. The first one simply requires you to list the parts of the assignment that you want students to be assessed on, then determine the weight for each section, and finally assign points based on their accuracy (see figure 14). Feedback in this case will be handwritten on the rubric page as you detail areas that necessitate improvement or praise. The second type of grading rubric is more complex and will take more time to develop, but the criteria are more descriptive and thus easier to use to give feedback to students (see table 7). Based on number of points they received, they will know exactly where they fell short or where they succeeded.

For additional examples, I encourage you to go online and search for rubrics and you will see a number of them available for you to adapt for your educational ministry context.

Criteria	Points Earned
Essay Content (10 points)	_____
Organization/ Structure (5 points)	_____
Graphic Illustrations (5 points)	_____
Overall writing quality and accuracy (5 points)	_____
Group Teamwork (5 points)	_____
Flow/On Topic Presentation (10 points)	_____
TOTAL (out of 40 points):	_____

Figure 14: Group Essay and Presentation Rubric (Simple)

Criteria					Points
	1	2	3	4	
Essay Content	Content is incomplete and major points are hard to discern. The essay has too many misconceptions	The student has a basic understanding of the topic, but some misconceptions exist. Some points weren't addressed.	All major points were stated, but not in great detail. Research is somewhat inadequate.	Student has a complete understanding of the topic and all major points are well researched and supported.	
Organization/ Structure	Little or no evidence of structure. The tone lacks description and detracts from the message.	Structure is inconsistent and hard to follow. Personal opinion was not present.	Adequate choice of words with a persuasive argument. The structure is generally acceptable.	Structure is clear and easy to follow. Essay is descriptive and has a persuasive tone with personal opinons.	
Group Teamwork (Group Grade)	Waisted time was evident. Group didn't work well together and failed to designate group roles.	Group roles were assigned, but not everyone participated (limited contribution).	Group members were coordinated but only provided moderate contributions.	All group members participated equally and helped each other as needed.	
On Topic Presentation (Group Grade)	Presentation lacked substance and enthusiasm. Group members stumbled over main concepts.	Utilized the alotted time limit. Each team member knew his or her responsibilities. Transitions were sloppy.	Information was presented in an organized fashion. Presentation included some details but not enough.	All group members spoke clearly and accurately. They were easy to understand.	
				Total	

Table 7: Group Essay and Presentation Rubric (Complex)

Conclusion

Howard Hendricks (1987) once wrote that the ultimate test of teaching (or preaching) is not what you do or how well you do it but what and how well the learner does. Good teachers and preachers can't be focused on what they do but on what their students are doing. Think about the piano or guitar teacher who is watching his or her student perform at a recital. The teacher can't perform for the student; it is the student's responsibility. That is one of the most frustrating parts of being a teacher. We want to help our students and give them hints that will ensure they do well because we care about their success, but we can't do that. They have to demonstrate that they can do it without our help. In your pursuit of student achievement, consider this quote from Tomlinson and Imbeau (2010): "Expert teachers don't just observe student behavior; they work to understand the affect that drives behavior so they can guide students in a positive direction" (p. 16). That in a nutshell is what assessment is all about. We, as Christian educators, have to figure out what is working and what is not working, what students know and what they don't know, where we can begin helping them without inhibiting them.

Are the people in your educational ministry progressing in their knowledge and application of God's Word? If you can't honestly answer that question, then I want to challenge you to apply the principles of this chapter. During your lessons, consider how you can implement formative assessments in your lesson to make sure students are following you and understanding your material as you progress through it. This can be done through quick checks, like having them give you a thumb up if they understand the material or by having students answer questions based on your content. Feel free to use variations of these or make up your own. At the end of your series of lessons, offer some kind of summative assessment for students to complete that will communicate to you whether or not your educational goals were met. If they were met, then move on to the next series of lessons, but if not, then go back and review to make sure everyone is on the same page before moving on.

After you have examined your students' assessments, be sure to provide them with useful feedback so they will know where they are and where they are going in the learning process (Earl, 2003). As Stiggins (1997) states, the communication mission of teachers involves two things: making sure that all message receivers understand the meaning of assessment results, and being sure that students are able to utilize those results effectively and efficiently to help themselves succeed. So make sure that communications takes place and time is given for students to reflect on the results. In this way, assessment will become part of the learning process as students internalize the insights that were given through feedback.

I'll close this chapter with something that I learned about teaching from one of my professors many years ago. He said that the more you know about your learners and the more you understand about the tools of the trade, the more effective of an educator you will be. The art of teaching involves bringing together the right tools for specific learners that is geared for specific content. That is what instructional design is all about. I hope and pray that in your pursuit of teaching biblical principles and beliefs, you will be able to apply these concepts in your specific educational ministry and see how a little extra effort on your part can help your students can flourish academically and spiritually.

Practice Makes Perfect

Effective Feedback Worksheet

Directions: Complete the table below adding assessments that you would like to use in your educational ministry context. Determine whether your tool is formative or summative, and then describe its purpose and how you will use it after the students have completed it. I have given you a few examples to get started.

Assessment Tool	Purpose	Use of Assessment
Weekly quizzes (formative assessments).	Measures if a student has gained enough information to succeed on summative assessment/test.	If a student fails a quiz, the teacher will go over the assessment with the student to determine where improvement is needed.
Oral question and answer at the end of class (formative assessment).	Measures skill areas such as speaking and reading.	If students get questions wrong, the teacher will review the material.
Final exam at the end of the course or unit of study (summative assessment).	To find out if a student knows enough information to go on to the next level.	If a student fails the final exam, he or she may need to repeat the course or get supplementary help.

Practice Makes Perfect

Lesson Plan Template

Directions: Use this template to create your own lesson plan.

- Title/Big Idea: _____

- Educational Goal(s):

- Lesson Context:

- Instructional Objectives:

- Detailed Lesson Procedures/Content to be Presented:

- Resources:

- Assessments and Reinforcements (Feedback):

Sources

Andrade, H. "Understanding Rubrics." *Saddleback.edu.* June 20, 2014. https://www.saddleback.edu/uploads/goe/understanding rubrics__by__heidi __goodrich __andrade.pdf

Dick, W. O., L. Carey, and J. O. Carey. *The Systematic Design of Instruction.* 7th ed. Englewood Cliffs, New Jersey: Merrill, 2011.

Earl, L. M. *Assessment as Learning: Using Classroom Assessment to Maximize Student Learning.* Thousand Oaks, California: Corwin Press, Inc., 2003.

Hendricks, H. *Teaching to Change Lives.* Colorado Springs, Colorado: Multnomah Books, 1987.

Kurtz, S. M., J. D. Silverman, and J. Draper. *Teaching and Learning Communication Skills in Medicine.* Boca Raton, Florida: CRC Press, 1998.

Marzano, R. J., D. J. Pickering, and J. E. Pollock. *Classroom Instruction That Works: Research-Based Strategies for Increasing Student Achievement.* Alexandria, Virginia: ASCD, 2001.

Stiggins, R. J. *Student-Centered Classroom Assessment.* Upper Saddle River, New Jersey: Prentice-Hall, Inc., 1997.

Tomlinson, C. A., and M. B. Imbeau. *Leading and Managing a Differentiated Classroom.* Alexandria, Virginia: ASCD, 2010.

Wiggins, G. *Educative Assessment: Designing Assessments to Inform and Improve Student Performance.* San Francisco, California: Jossey-Bass, 1998.

9
CONCLUSION

We need a new diagnosis of our students' inward
condition, one that is more perceptive
about their needs, less defensive about our own role in their plight,
and more likely to lead to creative modes of teaching.

—Parker Palmer

I will give you shepherds after my own heart,
who will lead you with knowledge and understanding.

—Jeremiah 3:15 (NIV)

"It was the best of times, it was the worst of times, it was the age of wisdom, it was the age of foolishness," penned Charles Dickens in the opening lines of his classic book *A Tale of Two Cities*. From the very onset of his story, Dickens used the rhetorical device of contrast to identify the struggles and differences between London and Paris. The book was set at a time when London, for the most part, was peaceful while Paris was splintering during its revolution in the late 1700s. It is widely believed that Dickens wrote this book in part because he wanted his readers to understand the dangers of a revolution if one ever occurred in England. The revolution in France had far-reaching consequences, as the book so poignantly exposed.

The authors of the Bible, much like Dickens, used past examples and stories as warnings for present and future generations. In fact, the apostle Paul used similar rhetorical reasoning in 1 Corinthians 10 as he demonstrated the importance of following God's instruction by using the people of Israel as a negative case study. At the beginning of the chapter, Paul wrote that all the Israelites ate the same spiritual food and drank the same spiritual drink, but yet God was not pleased with most of them. This was due to the fact that numerous Israelites had become idolaters, and others tested and Lord or participated in various kinds of wickedness. The Lord would not let their actions go unpunished, and at God's command, many were left to die in their sin. Interestingly, Paul asserted in 1 Corinthians 10:11–12 (NIV), "These things happened to them as examples and were written down as warnings for us, on whom the culmination of the ages has come. So if you think you are standing firm, be careful that you don't fall!" In this passage, Paul cautioned the people of Corinth not to follow in the footsteps of their predecessors. Instead, he wanted them to learn from Israel's mistakes and do the right thing the first time.

In a similar fashion, I want you to take note of some differences between two camps of people mentioned in the Bible and let their contrasting stories challenge you to persevere in your educational ministry. The first camp was laid out in the introduction of this book. If you recall, the Israelites, in the time of Ezekiel, listened to the prophet's words but neglected to put any of his instruction into practice. God told him in Ezekiel 33:31–32 that he was no more than a good entertainer to them. People came to hear him because he was amusing and fun to watch, but they refused respond to his messages.

Conversely, the New Testament tells us of another camp of people that did respond to the message of God. Listen to the apostle Paul's words in 1 Thessalonians 2:13 (NIV) as he describes the church in Thessalonica: "And we also thank God continually because, when you received the word of God, which you heard from us, you accepted it not as a human word, but as it actually is, the word of God, which is indeed at work in you who believe." If you have ever studied 1 Thessalonians, you will know that Paul spent a considerable amount of time in the context of this passage vindicating the character and ministry of those who shared the gospel in Thessalonica. He states in verses 1 through 12 that they are all witnesses to the fact that Paul and his companions were blameless in conduct, they didn't seek glory for themselves, and instead they only sought to encourage and exhort those in Thessalonica, sharing the Word of God to them. Then here in verse 13, he turns from talking about the characteristics of those who carried the gospel to those who received the gospel. He describes his thankfulness for how the Thessalonians entered into the Christian way of life.

One of the things that I love about this passage is Paul's use of the words *received* and *accepted*. Even though in our English language these words are pretty similar (they are synonyms), it is not so in Greek. They are actually two very different realities. The Greek word for *received* is *paralambano*, which means "to receive something transmitted from another." This word is used in the New Testament when talking about receiving a message or body of instruction or doctrine. Another example is in 1 Corinthians 11:23 when Paul says, "For I received from the Lord what I also passed on to you." One commentator compares this Greek word for receiving to signing a receipt at the post office so you can accept a package. It wasn't yours until you signed for it and took it as your own (Keathley, 2004). Likewise, Paul is saying here in 1 Thessalonians that their beliefs or doctrine about Jesus had become their own beliefs; they took possession of them just as that package would become the possession of the receiver.

But Paul recognized that there is a difference between simply receiving a message, believing it as truth, and actually living it out, and so Paul says that they accepted it too. The Greek word here for *accepted* is *dechomai*, which literally means "to receive in the sense of welcome." This word is used of welcoming a guest into one's home. It is a picture of hospitality. The first word meant that the message was delivered to them, but this second word means they welcomed it. The first word refers to "the hearing of the ear," while the second refers to "the hearing of the heart." John MacArthur (2002) adds that this means the Word of God was transferred from their minds to their hearts.

In this passage, Paul expresses his thankfulness (as any of us would be as teachers of God's Word) that the believers in Thessalonica "got it." They heard his words and allowed them to sink into their hearts. They accepted Paul's teaching because they knew his words were not just the words of men but of God. Interestingly, Paul does not end with discussing their acceptance of his teaching. He adds that this word is at work in their lives. The phrase "which is indeed at work in you" comes from the Greek word *energeo* from which we get our English word *energy* or *energize*. It really means "to work effectually, to work efficiently and productively." To this end, Keathley (2004) correctly surmises that when we receive and accept God's Word and welcome it by faith, it brings the power of God in our lives. This is not just a matter of the power of positive thinking, but the product of the miraculous work of the Holy Spirit in our lives.

Perhaps the *Tale of Two Cities*, for us as biblical instructors today, is not London and Paris like in Dickens's tale, but rather the ancient Israelites and first century Thessalonian Christians as we see them in the Bible. My hope is that their stories will challenge and exhort all of us as Christian educators to refuse to become satisfied with the status quo, with people coming to our meetings to watch a good show or be entertained, but instead we will seek our student's further engagement with the gospel (in and outside the learning environment) so it will be applied with great vigor and our city on a hill will not be hidden (Matthew 5:14).

Schlechty (2002) suggests that there are different levels of student engagement. For instance, a student who is only ritually engaged views educational assignments as having little or no real value to him or her. The student in this case will just listen to a lecture or do an assignment because it is expected or required. Other students may exhibit what Schlechty calls "retreatism." This is when a student is completely disengaged and refuses to expend any energy on anything the teacher says to do. Have you had students like these in your educational ministry? Maybe it's a spouse of a member in your group who obviously doesn't want to be there or several students in the youth group who only come because their parents make them attend. Whatever the case may be, our goal as educational ministers should be to help them see how meaningful learning can be. It is only then that they can become authentically engaged. Students who are authentically engaged see value and meaning in every lecture and assignment. Schlechty states that different types of engagement will produce different types of commitment and effort. Students who are ritually engaged will only learn what they have to so they will do well on an assessment. These students (and those who are completely disengaged) will obviously not retain as much information as they would if they were authentically engaged. So the question we must ask ourselves is: what can we do to help students become more authentically engaged?

I firmly believe that the principles of instructional design will help us in this pursuit, as focusing more on the instructional process will help produce students who have a genuine appetite for intellectual risk-taking and a desire to find the right answers and attain educational goals (Tomlinson and Imbeau, 2010). Instructional design helps us think about how we can supply students with opportunities to have their equilibriums become disturbed (intellectually speaking) so that they grasp just how important it is to dig deep into God's Word and apply it to their lives. Too many times, our students want to give up on searching for the truth in Scripture because it is seemingly too difficult. They look at the Old Testament prophets and think, *How can anyone understand this?* However, I hope we can be the kind of teachers who act as leaders in our unique learning environments as we challenge our students as the apostle Paul did in 2 Timothy 2:15 (NIV) when he stated, "Do your best to present yourself to God as one approved, a worker who does not need to be ashamed and who correctly handles the word of truth."

Phelps (2008) proposes that teachers actually have three roles as leaders: an advocate, an innovator, and a steward. As an advocate for student learning, teachers exhibit an ability to frame issues in a way that keeps students and learning as the central focus. This happens as they interact with students, parents (if the students are younger), and other teachers. Next, a teacher must know his or her role as an innovator. This implies that teachers are responsible for being change agents that transform programs by thinking outside of the box. Effective teachers are not afraid to make suggestions and implement new ideas and practices. They are always creative in their approach and in developing activities for students. Lastly, a teacher needs to be a good steward who shapes what happens in and out of the learning environment. According to Phelps, stewards are those who make positive changes to the teaching profession. They support and model professional growth and raise the level of effective education. In this, they serve as models of continued improvement. Applying this to educational ministries, your example should inspire other teachers in your context to do what they can to pursue greater student engagement, achievement, and application.

With that said, I want to return to something that I mentioned earlier in this book. Consider taking a team approach for your instructional design. Don't be a lone wolf when it comes to planning instruction, but instead work together and challenge other team members with new ideas, and be sure to assess not only your students but also your overall program on a regular basis. Also, don't be afraid to be evaluated as a teacher, but welcome constructive criticism. None of us have arrived as teachers. We can always learn and grow.

Before I close, let me quickly review the steps of instructional design that you can work on together as a team. The first step includes assuming responsibility for analyzing the characteristics of the learners (the target audience) and considering the context in which the instruction will be taught. This will include the tools that will be needed and the contexts in which the skills will eventually be used. The more teachers know about their students, the more appropriate the design of instruction will be (Dick, Carey, and Carey, 2009). Next, your team will conduct a needs analysis to measure the gaps between what your students already know and what they need to know. In this process, you will identify ideal characteristics of spiritual development, measure the noticeable gaps in your students, and then select and prioritize those gaps so you can decipher relevant topics to teach. Only after this is completed can you move on to step three, which includes focusing on the development of your main theme, essential questions, and educational goals. At the end of this step, you should have a good idea about how you will classify your educational goals (according to Bloom's Taxonomy) and how you will assess student learning at the end of your unit or course of study. The fourth step involves the scope and sequence of your instruction. Your scope includes what exactly will be taught during a given period of time. This will be based on the big ideas you garner from God's Word. Your sequence, on the other hand, will deal with the order in which your content will be presented. To establish this, you will need to decompose your learning tasks in order to see what steps are needed in order to reach your educational goals. Step five takes those decomposed learning tasks and creates instructional objectives for each lesson you will teach. These objectives should exhibit Mager's three-point emphasis of performance, conditions, and criteria. After this, you will be prepared for step six that asks you to expand your educational toolbox and create an organizational strategy that will display exactly how you will present your lessons (giving the overall framework) and a delivery strategy that will include the instructional mediums will be used during your lesson times. Hopefully, you will incorporate active learning techniques in your strategy that encourages active rather than passive learning. Lastly, the seventh and final step of your instructional design will include the development of summative and formative assessment that will be used to evaluate process in your students. Don't forget to give supportive feedback to students after you give them an assessment or assignment so they will be able to use those insights to further their education in the future. These seven steps are what instructional design is all about. I hope that you will be able to apply these principles into your normal routine as you prepare messages or lessons for your specific educational ministry. As I mentioned earlier, these concepts have revolutionized the way I look at educational ministry, and I know it can do the same for you.

I want to leave you with a quote from the late Howard Hendricks who once asked if ministers of the gospel were willing to pay the price for genuine development in their students. He stated, "There is, after all, a cost involved. Effective teaching isn't available at any bargain-basement sale. If you have the facts in view, I know you'll go ahead and gladly pay the cost. The thrill and fulfillment of effective teaching is just too satisfying to throw away in favor of limited living and lesser goals" (p. 130). Never sell yourself short when reaching for your full potential as an instructor in educational ministries. Always pursue excellence in both your teaching and design of instruction, to the glory of God!

Sources

Dick, W. O., L. Carey, and J. O. Carey. *The Systematic Design of Instruction*. 7th ed. Englewood Cliffs, New Jersey: Merrill, 2011.

Hendricks, H. *Teaching to Change Lives*. Colorado Springs, Colorado: Multnomah Books, 1987.

Keathley, J. H. "The Commendation and Thanksgiving (1 Thess. 2:13–20)." *Bible.org*. July 2, 2004. https://bible.org/seriespage/5-commendation-and-thanksgiving-1-thess-213-20.

MacArthur, J. *The Macarthur New Testament Commentary: 1 & 2 Thessalonians*. Chicago, Illinois: Moody Press, 2002.

Palmer, P. *The Courage to Teach: Exploring the Inner Landscape of a Teacher's Life*. San Francisco, California: Jossey-Bass, 2012.

Phelps, P. H. *Helping Teachers Become Leaders: The Clearing House*, 81 (2008): 119–122. Retrieved from EBSCO*host*.

Schlechty, P. C. *Working on the Work: An Action Plan for Teachers, Principals, and Superintendents*. San Francisco, California: Jossey-Bass Education, 2002.

Tomlinson, C. A., and M. B. Imbeau. *Leading and Managing a Differentiated Classroom*. Alexandria, Virginia: ASCD, 2010.

GLOSSARY

active learning techniques (ALTs): Modes of teaching that emphasize the importance of active verses passive learning. Teachers interact with students and provide opportunities that allow them to interact with one another and with the material so everyone is included.

big ideas: The ideas that bind each lesson together and help students make connections between each concept. They are the main concepts that biblical authors focus on and that teachers should pass on to their students.

Bloom's Taxonomy: Developed under the leadership of Benjamin Bloom, this taxonomy promotes higher forms of thinking in education. It includes a framework for classifying statements of what students are expected to learn as a result of instruction, and it helps teachers broaden a typical educational goal to embrace the promotion of knowledge transfer.

cooperative learning: Teaching strategies that allow students discuss the material with each other, help each other understand it, and encourage each other to work hard. Instead of the teacher being the main communicator of information, these strategies will allow students to discover the content for themselves and interact with it.

curriculum: Refers to the actual content, materials (e.g., books, videos, presentations, readings), and/or textbooks that teachers teach from. This also includes the concepts, ideas, and vocabulary that will be taught in the learning environment.

delivery strategy: Helps teachers determine what instructional mediums will be used (e.g., cooperative learning groups, drill and practice, reflective discussions, group presentations, debates, graphic organizers, etc.).

differentiation: An approach to teaching that considers the needs of every individual. It includes a teacher's proactive plan of instruction that consistently addresses the differences and needs that are seen in individual students. Every lesson is written or developed for the entire class, but each individual can also understand it. Teachers will differentiate the content (that which is taught), process (the sequence and instructional methods used), and product (what students know by the end of the course) of education.

duel-response survey: Uniquely designed to measure student perspectives about their *current* and *desired* performance levels. This is different that traditional single-response surveys in that it specifically provides clear data regarding the size, direction, and relative priority of performance gaps.

educational goals (also referred to as learning goals or terminal objectives): Statements of purpose or intention. They include the knowledge or skills learners should possess at the conclusion of an instructional unit or course. Educational goals are more general and less precise than instructional objectives. Instructional objectives are subparts of educational goals.

emotional intelligence: Involves our capacity to recognize our own emotions (as well as the emotions of those around us) and handle them or express them in healthy ways. This often manifests in the learning environment through a teacher's empathy, patience, and ability to balance student responsibility and teacher responsibility.

essential questions: Doorways through which teachers and students alike can explore the key concepts, themes, theories, issues, and problems that reside within the content. These push toward the heart or the essence of the subject matter and provide a lens through which all knowledge and activities will be processed.

expected student outcomes (also referred to as desired student outcomes): Statements that articulate what students are expected to know, feel, or do at the completion of their study in a particular program.

formative assessments: Assessments that are conducted during a term of learning to help the teacher determine where students are at in their understanding of certain concepts.

feedback: Communication from teachers that gives students direct and usable insights into their current performance after an assignment or assessment.

idea web: A graphic organizer that explains concepts by branching out into different levels. The main concept or theme is in the middle or the organizer, and concepts are branched out, it makes the organizer look like a spiderweb.

instructional design: Utilizes the principles of learning and instruction to plan for instructional materials, activities, information resources, and evaluation. The product will include instructional experiences that make the acquisition of knowledge and skills more palatable, which in turn will make the outcomes of instruction more observable and measurable.

instructional objectives: As subparts of educational goals, they form specific phrases that include a collection of words and/or pictures intended to display exactly what students will be expected to do as a result of instruction.

intelligence preference: The different intellectual abilities or hardwired aptitudes for learning or thinking that students possess. This involves a student's actual ability to learn.

jigsaw groups: A teaching strategy that encourages teachers to break down new concepts into segments that students (working in groups) can piece together like a jigsaw puzzle.

learning environment (also referred to as the learning context or educational ministry context): The physical and emotional context in which learning occurs.

learning outcome: Involves the kind of learning that will be required from students. Some learning tasks are substantially different from others in terms of amount and kind of cognitive effort required in learning.

learning profile: Includes the characteristics and needs of students. This will involve pertinent information about these five areas: their general characteristics (e.g., age, gender, cultural background), their interests, their learning style(s), their intelligence preference(s), and their spiritual maturity.

learning styles: A student's preferred way(s) in which he or she likes to take in and process information.

learning targets: Similar to instructional objectives, these student-friendly statements describe what students will learn and do during a particular lesson. This includes the lesson-sized chunk of learning that teachers expect their students to know. They are expressed from the student's point of view.

mnemonic devices: Techniques or strategies for improving or strengthening memory. The idea behind mnemonic devices is to help students learn to recall concepts by thinking of a memorable sentence. The first letter of each word in the sentence, when put together, forms the mnemonic.

needs assessment: Involves a "gap analysis" of the existing knowledge and performance of students. This analysis lists the gaps between desired and actual levels of student performance in a particular educational program. The goal is to find areas in which a large number of students are experiencing difficulty in and for which they are not already receiving quality instruction.

nonlinguistic representation strategies: Teaching strategies that challenge students to generate mental pictures that go along with the information they are learning and then crafting graphic representations of that information.

organizational strategy: Helps teachers sequence the chosen content that is to be presented and determine how that content will be presented. This is the overall framework of the lesson and how the lesson is organized.

power-thinking graphic organizer: A graphic organizer that allow learners to organize ideas and information hierarchically. It can be used to group terms, ideas, and vocabulary words into main headings and subheadings (much like an outline but in visual form).

reflective journaling: Allows students to reflect or contemplate on the thoughts or feelings they have toward a text or a concept they are learning during a lecture. Students' personal thoughts or responses help them to develop a personal connection with the material and their own writing.

rubrics: Scoring tools that communicate expectations for an assignment to students. Specifically, they list the criteria for an assignment and articulate gradations of quality for each criterion, from excellent to poor.

summative assessments: The evaluations of students at the end of the course or class to gauge whether or not all the educational goals and instructional objectives have been met.

scope and sequence of instruction: The scope of instruction involves what exactly will be taught during a given period of time. The sequence of instruction, on the other hand, has to do with the order in which the content will be presented.

sketch noting: A relatively new graphic organizer that utilizes current technology (e.g., iPads and other tablets) to take notes with diagrams, charts, and/or drawings.

student readiness: Includes the knowledge, understandings, and abilities students already have in relation to the content. If some students are not ready for certain concepts, instructors will have to spend time at the beginning of the unit filling in background knowledge.

Venn diagrams: A graphic organizer composed of two overlapping circles, where each side represents differences and the middle represents the similarities between the two.

zone of proximal development: Areas of learning in which students require interaction or support from others (e.g., teachers and/or peers) in order to attain expertise. These areas include concepts or skills in which students have the potential to grasp or develop in but can't quite do it on their own yet. They require the assistance of more competent peers or teachers.

Printed in the United States
By Bookmasters